CORPORATE GOVERNANCE
ISSUES AND CHALLENGES

CORPORATE GOVERNANCE
ISSUES AND CHALLENGES

Edited by

Dr. Suman Kalyan Chaudhury

M.Com, MBA, PGDPM & IR, Ph.D.
Reader cum Placement Officer
Department of MBA
Berhampur University
Berhampur
(Odisha)

DISCOVERY PUBLISHING HOUSE PVT. LTD.
NEW DELHI-110 002

Published by:
Tilak Wasan

DISCOVERY PUBLISHING HOUSE PVT. LTD.
4383/4A, Ansari Road, Darya Ganj
New Delhi-110 002 (India)
Phone : +91-11-23279245, 43596064-65
Fax : +91-11-23253475
E-mail : parul.wasan@gmail.com
discoverypublishinghouse@gmail.com
web : www.discoverypublishinggroup.com

***First Edition:* 2012**

ISBN: 978-93-5056-051-8

Corporate Governance: ***Issues & Challenges***

Printed at:
Shree Balaji Art Press
Delhi

Preface

Corporate governance has assumed vital role and significance due to globalization and liberalization. With the opening of economy and to be in line with WTO requirements, if the Indian corporates have to survive and succeed amidst increasing competition globally, it can only be through transparency in operations. The excellence in terms of customer satisfaction, in terms of return, in terms of product and service, in terms of return to promoters and in terms of social responsibilities towards society and people cannot be achieved without practicing good corporate governance.

Business world is, to an extent, a reflection of the country's social and cultural ethos. The unprincipled behaviour among people has become so commonplace that even the corporate world has been affected. It is; therefore, felt that unless companies look after the interests of their stakeholders and apply the ethical code of conduct in their dealings, they can at best gain only temporary benefits. Companies have begun to realize the importance of good Corporate Governance and Business Ethics. It is evidence from the Global Investor Opinion Survey Key Findings of McKinsey & Company, July 2002 that the companies with good corporate governance mechanisms have performed better as compared to companies with poor governance records. Therefore it would be advisable to restructure and redesign the corporate governance codes to meet the global changes to tone up the performance and investor confidence of the company.

This book is an attempt to present and explain the various issues and challenges for implementing corporate governance practices in Indian corporate world. It is hoped that the book will be use to researchers, shareholders, corporate, governments, banks and academicians as a whole.

DR. SUMAN KALYAN CHAUDHURY

Acknowledgements

Every action requires an initiator, influencer. I am initiated into writing this book, primarily, by the inspiration provided by my students and friends in the same profession. My colleagues are always stand with for support and cheering me. Therefore, I can't but gratefully acknowledge my indebtedness to all those who have extended generous assistance in the successful accomplishment of this indispensable work .It will be a serious blunder if I forget to mention some of my colleagues Prof. Niranjan Nayak , Centre Head, Koustav Business School, Dr. Kirti Ranjan Swain, Associate Prof., IPSAR Business School, Cuttack, Dr. Ashok Kumar Panigrahi, Asst. Prof., RITEE Business School, Raipur, Prof. Ashok Kumar Panda, Dean, Astha School of Management for their ardent encouragement and beacon guidance in bringing out this work.

I profusely thank my Chairman of the institute, Er. Sundhansu Kumar Dash for his rock support and continuous push that furthered my efforts seamlessly towards quick accomplishment. My heartfelt gratitude to him.

Last but not least my heartfelt gratitude to my wife Sinu knows no bounds for her immaculate co-operation. Needless to depict, I am indebted to my family members for their love and affection and inspired me in my problem solving while in action.

I am also much beholden to Mr.Tilak Wasan, Managing Director, Discovery Publishing House Pvt. Ltd., New Delhi for publishing the work in a record time.

DR. SUMAN KALYAN CHAUDHURY

Contents

Contributors

Dr. Ashok Kumar Panigrahi, Associate Professor, Dept. of Commerce and Management, REET School of Management, Raipur, Chhattisgarh.

Dr. Arvinda. S, Professor, Dept.of Management, College of Business and Economics, Adi-Haqi Campus, Mekelle University, P.O. Box:451, Mekelle, Tigray, Ethiopia.

Dr. Suman Kalyan Chaudhury, M.Com, MBA, PGDPM & IR, Ph.D., Reader cum Placement Officer, Department of MBA., Berhampur University, Berhampur, (Odisha).

Dr. Jagdish. R. Raiyani, Asst. Prof, Faculty of Management, Shree Maharshi Dayanand Saraswati MBA College, Tankara, Rajkot, Gujarat.

Dr. Sudhansu Kumar Das, Lecturer in Commerce,V.N (Auto) College, Jajpur Road, Orissa.

Dr. Santosh Singh Bais, Assistant Professor, Dept. of Commerce & Management Government. First Grade College, Chincholi-585307, Karnataka.

Dr. Fisseha Girmay Tessema, Assistant Professor, Department of Accounting & Finance, College of Business & Economics, Mekelle University, Mekelle, Ethiopia.

Dr. Kirti. Ranjan Swain, Asst. Prof, IPSAR B- School, Cuttack, Orissa.

Dr. Simanchala Das, Asst. Prof., Global Institute of Business Management, Bhubaneswar, Orissa.

Dr. Hailay Gebretinsae, Head & Asst. Professor, Dept.of Management, College of Business & Economics, Mekelle University, Mekelle, Ethiopia.

Dr. Veershetty G Rathod, Assistant Professor, Department of Commerce & Management, Sahyadri Arts & Commerce College, Kuvempu University, Shimoga-577203, Karnataka.

Dr. Niranjan Nayak, Centre Head, Koustuv Business School, Bhubaneswar, Orissa.

Mr. Siddharth Shankar Kanungo, Assistant Professor (Finance), Bhavan's Centre for Communication & Management, Bhubaneswar, Orissa.

Mr. Susanta Kumar Mishra, District Project Manager, Targeted Rural Initiative for Poverty Termination and Infrastructure, District Rural Development Agency, Panchayati Raj Dept., Government of Orissa.

1

Corporate Governance

Issues and Challenges in Indian Corporate World

Dr. Ashok Kumar Panigrahi
Dr. Suman Kalyan Chaudhury

Abstract

While corporate governance may not dictate the economic prospects of developing countries, it certainly plays an integral role in shaping them. India's corporate-governance framework is sophisticated for a developing country. However, considerable room remains for improvement. Most notably, India must reform how its boards of directors function, improve its enforcement mechanisms, redefine its corporate laws and embrace corporate governance as a philosophy. In this chapter an attempt is made to highlight the main areas where there exist loopholes in the prevailing system, suggestive measures to make the corporate governance system effective and efficient.

Introduction

Corporate Governance can be understood to be a systematic process by which Companies are directed & controlled to ensure that they are managed in the manner that meets stakeholders' aspirations and societal expectation. This leads to the corporate governance philosophies of: Trusteeship; Transparency; Empowerment and Accountability; Control and Ethical Corporate Behaviour.

'Corporate Governance' encompasses commitment to values and to ethical business conduct to maximize shareholder values on a sustainable basis, while ensuring fairness to all stakeholders including customers, employees, and investors, vendors, Government and society at large. Corporate Governance is the system by which companies are directed and managed. It influences how the objectives of the company are set and achieved, how risk is monitored and assessed and how performance is optimized. Sound Corporate Governance is therefore critical to enhance and retain investors' trust.

Corporate governance is all about ethical conduct in business. Ethics is concerned with the code of values and principles that enables a person to choose between right and wrong, and therefore, select from alternative courses of action. Further, ethical dilemmas arise from conflicting interests of the parties involved. In this regard, managers make decisions based on a set of principles influenced by the values, context and culture of the organization. Ethical leadership is good for business as the organization is seen to conduct its business in line with the expectations of all stakeholders. What constitutes good Corporate Governance will evolve with the changing circumstances of a company and must be tailored to meet these circumstances. There is therefore no one single model of Corporate Governance.

Corporate Governance in India

India has comprehensive laws governing corporate governance. The Companies Act, 1956 covers corporate governance widely through its various provisions such as inclusion of directors' responsibility statement in the directors' report under Section 217(2AA), constitution of audit committee under Section 292A fixing maximum ceiling on remuneration that can be drawn by a director under Schedule XIII, and those relating to oppression, mismanagement, etc. Further, environmental and other pieces of legislation also protect different stakeholders' interest, ensuring, in the process, good corporate governance. As a result of the interest generated in the corporate sector by the Cadbury Committee's report, the issue of Corporate Governance was studied in depth and dealt with by the Confederation of Indian Industries (CII), the

Associated Chamber of Commerce and the Securities and Exchange Board of India (SEBI).

The Confederation of Indian Industry (CII) published India's first comprehensive code on corporate governance (Desirable Corporate Governance: A Code) in 1998. This was followed by the recommendations of the Kumar Mangalam Birla Committee on Corporate Governance. This committee was appointed by the Securities and Exchange Board of India (SEBI). The recommendations were accepted by SEBI in December 1999, and are now enshrined in Clause 49 of the Listing Agreement of every Indian stock exchange. SEBI also instituted a committee under the chairmanship of Mr. N. R. Narayana Murthy which recommended enhancements in corporate governance. SEBI has incorporated the recommendations made by the Narayana Murthy Committee on Corporate Governance in Clause 49 of the listing agreement. The revised Clause 49 has been made effective from January 1, 2006. In addition, the Department of Company Affairs, Government of India, constituted a nine-member committee under the chairmanship of Mr. Naresh Chandra, former Indian ambassador to the U.S., to examine various corporate governance issues in 2002.

In India corruption is an all embracing phenomenon. In this, if the respective players in the field were to adopt healthy principles of good corporate governance and avoid corruption in their transactions, India could really take a step forward to becoming a less corrupt country and improving its rank in the Corruption Perception Index listed by the Transparency International.

Studies in India and abroad show that markets and investors take notice of well managed companies respond positively to them and reward such companies with higher valuations. A common feature is that they have systems in place, which allow sufficient freedom to Board and Management to take decisions towards progress and to innovate, while remaining within the framework of effective accountability. In other words they have a good system of corporate governance. Strong corporate governance is indispensable to resilient and vibrant capital markets and is an important instrument of investor protection. Securities and Exchange Board of India constituted a Committee on Corporate Governance under the Chairmanship of Mr. Kumar Mangalam Birla. The committee observed that there are companies, which have set high standards of governance while there are many more whose practices are matters of concern. There is increasing concern about standards of financial reporting and accountability especially after losses are suffered by investors and leaders in the recent past, which could have been avoided with better and more transparent reporting practices. Companies raise capital from market and investors suffered due to unscrupulous managements that performed much worse than past reported figures. Bad governance was also exemplified by allotment of promoters' share at preferential prices disproportionate to market value, affecting minority holders' interests. Many corporate did not pay heed to investors' grievances. While there were enough rules and regulations to take care of grievances, yet the inadequate implementation and the absence of severe penalty left much to be desired. The Kumar Mangalam Committee made mandatory and non-mandatory recommendations. Based on the recommendations of this Committee, a new clause 49 was incorporated in the Stock Exchange Listing Agreements ("Listing Agreements"). The important aspects, in brief, are:

(i) Board of Directors is accountable to shareholders;

(ii) Board controls are laid down code of conduct and accountable to shareholders for creating, protecting and enhancing wealth and resources of the Company reporting promptly in transparent manner while not involving in day to day management;

(iii) Classification of non-executive directors into those who are independent and those who are not;

(iv) Independent directors not to have material or pecuniary relations with the Company/subsidiaries and if had, to disclose in Annual Report;

(*v*) Laying emphasis on caliber of non-executive directors especially independent directors;

(*vi*) Sufficient compensation package to attract talented non-executive directors;

(*vii*) Optimum combination of not less than 50 per cent of non-executive directors and of which companies with non-executive Chairman to have at least one third of independent directors and under executive Chairman at least one half of independent directors;

(*viii*) Nominee directors to be treated on par with any other director;

(*ix*) Qualified independent Audit committee to be set-up with minimum of three all being non-executive directors with one having financial and accounting knowledge;

(x) Corporate governance report to be part of Annual Report and disclosure on directors' remuneration etc., to be included;

Naresh Chandra Committee recommendations relate to the Auditor-Company relationship and the role of Auditors. Report of the SEBI Committee on Corporate Governance recommended that the mandatory recommendations on matters of disclosure of contingent liabilities, CEO/CFO Certification, definition of Independent Director, independence of Audit Committee and independent director exemptions in the report of the Naresh Chandra Committee, relating to corporate governance, be implemented by SEBI. Narayana Murthy Committee recommendations include role of Audit Committee, Related party transactions, Risk management, compensation to Non- Executive Directors, Whistle Blower Policy, Affairs of Subsidiary Companies, Analyst Reports and other non-mandatory recommendations.

When it comes to corporate governance, we think we will have to look at the hardware as well as the software aspect. So far as the software aspect is concerned, we would suggest, it depends on the values cherished and practiced by the members of the Board of Directors as well as the management of an organization. It is always possible to mouth very high principles but act in a very lowly manner. If there is going to be divergence between practice and precept, then we are not going to achieve good corporate governance. This is the first point to be realized.

The most important aspect for observing corporate governance is the top management, particularly the board of directors and the senior level management of an enterprise–walking their talk. It is by walking their talk that the top management can earn credibility. This also has a direct bearing on the morale of an organization. When it comes to the hardware aspect of corporate governance, we go into the issue of a code, which becomes a reference point for behaviour. But the sad fact in our country is that even though there is a lot of talk about corporate governance, when it comes to reality, nothing much happens. With the SEBI trying to bring some discipline in the stock market especially in terms of greater transparency and disclosure norms, corporate governance in the Indian context at least seems to focus primarily and rightly on the issue of transparency. It is lack of transparency that leads to corrupt or illegal behaviour. If corporate governance is concerned with better ethics and principles, it is only natural that the focus should be on transparency. But how is this transparency to be achieved? One method of course is the code. Another would be the regulatory authorities like SEBI, RBI etc. laying down guidelines so that a certain degree of transparency is automatically ensured. Another legal approach to achieve better corporate governance may be to look at the whole issue of bringing the corporate sector under the discipline of debt and equity. Perhaps amendment of the Companies Act and bringing in this discipline will also help in automatically ensuring better ethics and corporate governance.

Issues and Challenges in Indian CG System

Perhaps the most important challenge we face towards better corporate governance is the mindset of the people and the organizational culture. This change will have to come from within. The government or the regulatory agencies at best can provide certain environment, which will be conducive for such a mindset taking place, but the primary responsibility, is of the people especially the members of the board of directors and the top management. Another important aspect is to realize that ultimately the spirit of corporate governance is more important than the form. Substance is more important than style. Values are the essence of corporate governance and these will have to be clearly articulated and systems and procedures devised, so that these values are practiced. We then come to a common moral problem in running enterprises. One can have practices which are legal but which are unethical. In fact, many a time, tax planning exercises may border on the fine razor's edge between the strictly legal and the patently unethical. A clear understanding of the fundamental values which govern corporate governance and their explicit articulation in a proper code backed by well established structures and traditions like the ethics committee and audit committee may be the best insurance for good corporate governance under the circumstances.

Corporate governance and ethical behaviour have a number of advantages. Firstly, they help to build good brand image for the company. Once there is a brand image, there is greater loyalty, once there is greater loyalty, there is greater commitment to the employees, and when there is a commitment to employees, the employees will become more creative. In the current competitive environment, creativity is vital to get a competitive edge.

Suggestive Measures for an Effective CG System

These are the few steps which we feel necessary for effective corporate governance which can also act as preventive measures to restrict the malpractices in corporate governances. For that every company is expected to:

- Recognize and publish the respective roles and responsibilities of board and management
- Have a board of an effective composition, size and commitment to adequately discharge its responsibilities and duties

- Actively promote ethical and responsible decision-making
- Have a structure to independently verify and safeguard the integrity of the company's financial reporting
- Promote timely and balanced disclosure of all material matters concerning the company
- Respect the rights of shareholders and facilitate the effective exercise of those rights
- Establish a sound system of risk oversight and management and internal control
- Fairly review and actively encourage enhanced board and management effectiveness
- Ensure that the level and composition of remuneration is sufficient and reasonable and that its relationship to corporate and individual performance is defined.
- Recognize legal and other obligations to all legitimate stakeholders.
- Corporate Governance Rating be made mandatory for listed companies.

Openness, integrity and accountability are the key elements of Corporate Governance for any corporate entity. These factors assume greater importance in case of Public Sector Banks. It is, therefore, necessary that the Board of Directors, external auditors and supervisors of bank strive to achieve greater degree of openness, transparency, integrity and accountability in the working of the institution. Banks deal in trust. If trust is in suspicion, damaged or lost, the resulting financial loss cannot measure the true risk. Trust being the foundation of banking, the discussion over applicability of good governance has really been a non-issue. Good governance and practices are synonymous to banking, banks and bankers. The essence of Corporate Governance is a framework of effective accountability to all stakeholders. Corporate Governance is an instrument for benefiting all stakeholders of a corporate entity. In its widest sense, Corporate Governance is almost akin to a trusteeship. It is about creating an outperforming organization, which leads to increasing customer satisfaction and shareholder value. A code for corporate governance for public sector banks in India could be in the form of a set of prescriptions and proscriptions for the key decision makers of a bank-I its Chairman, Executive and non-Executive Directors, institutional investors and external auditors. Such a code, it is believed, would enable the Boards of the banks to resolve conflict of interests between shareholders, customers, employees and other stakeholders. An informed debate on the issue of contemporary banking in the board rooms would help develop the vision to imagine crises and the will to act pre-emptively. In a deregulated milieu, the Public Sector Banks are bound to demand, and rightly so, greater functional autonomy for flexibility in decision making. Such autonomy, however, needs to be accompanied by greater accountability on the part of their Boards to the stakeholders. A Code of Corporate Governance could be an effective instrument for achieving this goal.

The Reserve Bank of India has set up various working groups to evaluate its existing corporate governance norms for banks. The Khan Working Group Report, though it did not deal with corporate governance per se, recommended full operational autonomy and flexibility to the management and boards of banks. The Narasimham Committee I recommended a gradual progress towards BIS norms and suggested the ending of the dual control over the sector by the RBI and the Ministry of Finance. The Narasimham Committee II (1998) recommended reducing government control and strengthening of internal controls. Additionally, Dr. Patil Advisory Group and Varma Group have made recommendations on international best practices of Corporate Governance for banking companies. The report of the Consultative Group of Directors of Banks/Financial Institutions—chaired by A.S. Ganguly—has tackled the issues of ethics, transparency and corporate governance. It has focussed on more fundamental issues like the supervisory role of boards of banks and financial institutions and functioning of the boards vis-à-vis compliance, transparency, disclosures, audit committees etc. A governance framework must include effective systems of Control and Accountability, and above all responsible attitudes on the part of those handling public money. It is important that the drive to provide improved services at reduced costs should be maintained and that this drive should not be stifled. At such time it is even more essential to maintain honesty in the spending of public money and to ensure that the traditional public sector values are not neglected in the effort to maximize economy and efficiency.

Ethics in managing an organization are vital for long term survival. It is defined as disciplined dealing with what is good and what is bad and what are moral duties and obligations. As far as business ethics are concerned, a minimum code of ethics has to be practiced in competition, public relations and social responsibilities. Corporate Governance encourages ethical standards and sound business practices. Corporate governance extends beyond corporate law. Its objective is not mere fulfillment of legal requirements but ensuring commitment on managing transparently for maximizing shareholder values. As competition increases, technology pronounces the deal of distance and speeds up communication, environment also changes. In this dynamic environment the systems of Corporate Governance also need to evolve, upgrade in time with the rapidly changing economic and industrial climate of the country. Finally the key lesson for us to learn is that Regulations and Policies are only one part of improving governance. Existence of a comprehensive system alone cannot guarantee ethical pursuit of shareholder's interest by Directors, officers and employees. Quality of governance depends upon competence and integrity of Directors, who have to diligently oversee the management while adhering to impeachable ethical standards. Strengthened systems and enhanced transparency can only further the ability. Transparency about a company's governance process is critical. Implementing Corporate Governance structures are Important but instilling the right culture–work culture is Most Essential.

Corporate Governance in the Public Sector cannot be avoided and for this reason it must be embraced. But

Corporate Governance should be embraced because it has much to offer to the Public Sector. Good Corporate Governance, Good Government and Good Business go hand in hand.

Common Sense Approach of Effective Corporate Governance

Excessive regulation stifles innovation and growth, which is also a major risk. Shareholder activism needs to be encouraged, or at least not stifled. They are the nest check on fraudulent practices of managers and directors. Regulation may have to be tightened, if a scam is sensed, but they can always be rolled back or slackened. As regards the pressure on managers, they should consult the board, as often as they have to in order to fully apprise themselves of the pros and cons of any strategy. The board members, in return, should ensure free space to executive management. The board members should lead by example. They must set the benchmarks of professionalism and ethics, to be followed in the company. If they can't keep up with the pace of the dynamic business environment, then they should quite gracefully. The art of corporate governance lies in establishing convergence between interests of managers and other stakeholders and selecting boards that provide this crucial link, ensuring that managers do not abuse their authority nor feel cramped to such an extent that they feel rusted. As one author has aptly put it "if corporate governance is practiced, like fidelity in marriage with the sole objective of not being caught while cheating, the clearly, it would remain as rocky as a marriage". So a voluntary effort is the need of the hour. It's a myth to think and believe that 'we are only like that', this attitude must be overcome. Integrity and honesty never go un-rewarded, so patience and perseverance are very important. Intense competition and globalization has its plus points too. It has helped improve the position of investors and has helped push the National Stock markets to new highs, never experienced before. The government has taken bold steps to upgrade the Indian investment environment to global standards.

Conclusion

Effectiveness of a system of corporate governance cannot be legislated by law nor can any system of corporate governance be static. In an energetic and lively environment, systems of corporate governance need to be continually evolved. The Narayan Murthy committee believes that its recommendations raise standards of corporate governance and make them attractive for domestic and global capital. These recommendations can also form the base for further evolution of the structure of corporate governance in consonance with the rapidly changing economic and industrial environment of the country in the new millennium. One valuable suggestion, given by the Hampel Committee, but which holds just as good for India is that the boards should consider introducing procedures for assessing their own collective performance and that of the individual directors. A crucial consideration which must not be overlooked is that though the regulatory bodies have brought out various guidelines and rules to ensure corporate governance, it is largely an issue of ethic, and hence difficult to enforce. It must come from within the organization. Thus, corporate governance largely depends on the following: The quality of the promoters, the intentions of the promoters, the systems and procedures adopted the transparency in the activities, and the quality of persons at the helm of day-to-day affairs. Every person associated with the company must appreciate the need for corporate governance, which cannot be achieved by merely asking the company to do various things. Corporate governance is a self-regulation and cannot be imposed.

2

Corporate Governance
The New Mantra

Dr. Santosh M. Singh

Abstract

Corporate governance has become the latest buzzword in the corporate sector in India. Kumaramanglam Birla was recently quoted as saying that the principal objective of good corporate governance is to enhance value. Stakeholder corporate governance is a system that effectively enforces accountability relationships between the executive management and the board of directors and also between the board of directors and shareholders of a company. Corporate governance assumes importance for publicity traded companies because of the separation between the management and the shareholders. This separation gives rise to the classic agency problem. Therefore, corporate governance system primarily addresses the agency problem. In the age of competitive Globalization and dynamic world, business enterprises need to focus on innovative practices which will help in maximizing stake and shareholders wealth. The fundamental concern of corporate governance is to ensure that the firm's directors and mangers act ethically in the interests of the firm and its shareholders and that the mangers are held accountable to capital providers for the use of assets. The concept of corporate governance can be taken as a parallel to the quality practices under the ISO standard. It also involves entry of non-executive directors into the board, and making the members more positive and dynamic in their activities. All business information must be made available to them, and system controls are activated to ensure authenticity, timeliness and effectiveness of information. The basic principles of corporate of corporate governance are based on ethical parameters such as complete transparency, integrity and accountability. The present paper addresses the issues of corporate performance, transparency, strategies, executive functions, compensation and accountability, auditors and several related issues.

Key Words: Maytas, governance, corporate, transparency, accountability, globalization.

Introduction

Corporate governance is the new buzzword or rather a concept in corporate management that is yet to catch up in India but that has the potential to significantly improve corporate performance. In the case of corporate governance shareholders is considered as God. Corporate governance has assumed significance in India because it has been given importance by institutions like World Bank, ADB, OECD etc. The focus on improving corporate governance and enhancing shareholder wealth is relatively new in India. Earlier, the managements were least concerned with how the shareholders were benefited from the company's performance. The role of company was to pay dividends and hold AGM. There was minimum communication between company management and shareholders. Investors had to depend on news reports to get information about their companies. But all these have changed now.

In those days when business used to be small, the owner and the manager were one and the same. Years later when the businesses increased in size with the advent of the joint stock organization there emerged a need to have two distinct and separate entities, one for management and the other to protect and further the owner's interest, on other worlds to 'Govern the Corporation'. Thus emerged the concept of corporate governance–a system by which companies are directed and governed. In order for a corporation to perform well the manger should be both 'able' and 'accountable'.

Corporate governance is rightly understood as putting people at the forefront of business, because all business must be fundamentally a matter of people rather than machines, products or even money. Good corporate governance has been sought to be implemented by attending to long term strategic goals, employees, community and environment, customers and suppliers, and compliance with laws and regulations. When seen deeply these various elements have one common theme running through them–that of being attentive to and conscious of ethical treatment of people in their various relations with the corporation. The ideal situation would, therefore, be when all parties are given equal share of corporate decision making.

History of Corporate Governance

The seeds of modern Corporate Governance were probably sown by the Watergate Scandal in the United States. As a result of subsequent investigations, US regulatory and legislative bodies were able to highlight the control failures that had allowed several major Corporations to make illegal political contributions and to bribe government officials. This led to the development of the Foreign and Corrupt Practices Act of 1977 in USA that contained specific provisions regarding the establishment, maintenance and review of systems of internal control. This was followed in 1979 by the Securities and Exchange Commission of USA's proposals for mandatory reporting on internal financial controls. In 1985, following series of high profile business failures in the USA. The most notable one of which being the Savings and Loan collapse, the Tread way Commission was formed. Its primary role was to identify the main causes of misrepresentation in Financial Reports and to recommend ways of reducing incidence thereof. The Tread way Report published in 1987 highlighted the need for aproper control environment, independent Audit Committees and an objective Internal Audit function. It called for published reports on the effectiveness of internal control. It also requested the sponsoring organizations to develop an integrated set of internal control criteria to enable companies to improve their controls. Accordingly COSO (Committee of

Sponsoring Organizations) was born. The report produced by it in1992 stipulated a control framework, which has been endorsed and refined in the four subsequent UK reports: Cadbury, Rutteman, Hampel and Turnbull. While developments in the United States stimulated a debate in the UK , a spate of scandals and collapses in that country in the late 1980s and early 1990's led the Shareholders and Banks to worry about their investments. These also led the Government in UK to recognize that the then existing legislation and self-regulation were not working. The issue of corporate governance became particularly significant in the context of globalization because one special feature of the late 20th century/21 st century globalization is that in addition to the traditional three elements of the economy, namely physical capital in terms of plant and machinery, technology and labour, the volatile element of financial capital invested in the emerging markets and in the third world countries is an important element of modern globalization and has become particularly powerful. Thanks to the ubiquitous application of information technology, at the touch of a computer mouse, it is possible now to transfer billions of dollars across borders. The significance and the impact of the volatility of the financial capital was realized when in June 1997 the currency of South East Asian countries started melting down in countries like Thailand, Indonesia, South Korea and Malaysia. It was realized by the World Bank and all investors that it is not enough to have good corporate management but one should have also good corporate governance because the investors want to be sure that the decisions taken are ultimately in the interest of all stakeholders. Honesty is the best policy is a fact that is now being re-discovered. In practical terms, corporate governance has meant that there should be at the board level non-official directors who are professionals and who have no conflicting interests and who can particularly operate the two key committees, the Ethics Committee and the Finance Committee to see that there is greater transparency in the management of the enterprise. Corporate governance ultimately has to come to mean better transparency in the operations without sacrificing business strategy or business secrets which are necessary for success in the marketplace, and absolutely ethical behaviour where the conduct of the company will not only be legal but also ethical.

Concept of Corporate Governance

Corporate Governance is an integrated framework whereby people formally organise themselves for a defined purpose, and they apply critical processes consistently to achieve predicted performance for sustainable development. It is well accepted world over that Corporate Governance is critical for making competitive enterprises, improving industrial performance, creating jobs and sustainable development. Corporate Governance has thus become the most debated topic in last 15 years. There are different perceptions and beliefs around the world about corporate governance and in all this corporate governance have become a rhetoric only. Much debated principles of corporate governance like independent directors, audit committees, control on related party transactions and Investor protection cannot ensure corporate sustainability and hence corporate governance has remained a rhetoric only far from reality. The economic boundaries are vanishing and a Computer Mouse has become mightier than the sword and pen. The power of information is now in hands of *People.* Now people can evaluate corporate *Performance* on hundreds of parameters. On click of a mouse people change their investment portfolio, their jobs and buy the best product available anywhere in the world. Power of information has also increased competition, which is now not restricted to attracting customers, but it is more intense in attracting talent and financiers, without which companies can't stand at all. Therefore it is critical that companies must have well defined *Process* to consistently achieve predicted results year after year. Corporate strategies and management practices are taken as given, and business ethics has become a competitive success factor. Good people associate with the companies which have a well defined *Purpose* in the form of vision and stakeholder policies and sincere efforts are put to fulfil those commitments in long run.

What is Corporate Governance All About?

In Academics, corporate governance refers to an economic, legal and institutional environment that allows companies to diversify, grow, restructure and exist, and do everything necessary to maximize long term shareholders value.

Adrian Cadbury defines "Corporate governance is the system by which companies are directed and controlled"

The Institute of Directors (UK) "Effective corporate governance ensures that long term strategic objectives and plans are established, and that the proper management and management structure are in place to achieve these objectives, while at the same time making sure that the structure functions to maintain the corporate integrity, reputation, and accountability to its relevant constituencies".

In short, corporate governance should be recognized as a set of standards which aims to improve the company's image, efficiency, effectiveness and social responsibility. It is simply no longer enough to comply with legal requirements. In one line, the relationship between the owners and managers in directing and controlling companies as separate legal entities. Corporate governance at the highest level is about the Board of Directors.

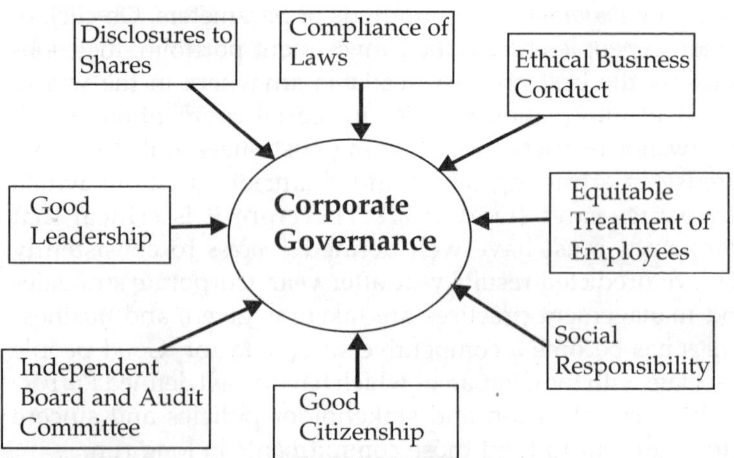

Corporate Governance: The New Mantra

The age old Ricardian Theory of Competitive Advantage has been replaced by very many theories on competition and co-existence among the competitors leading to a new coinage, 'co-appetition' by Ray Noorda of Novell Software in 1993. The phrase corporate governance is of recent vintage. According to Bob Tricker there term come to the fore in early 1980s in the United States during the heydays of the corporate takeovers.

The major driving forces behind the changes were the collapse of anti-capitalist political ideologies, technology and its impact substantially contributed for the change in investor attitude and the investors were convinced that only good governance leads to good performance and the corporates have a responsibility towards the society as good 'Corporate Citizens' in this context it is worth mentioning that for the first time in India the 'Corporate Citizen Award for school Relevance' was conferred on the Infosys Foundation. Corporate governance also aims at enhancing the value for both the shareholders and the stakeholders and also ensures the proper growth of the capital market in an economy.

Studies by some of the leading management consultancies attributed the reasons for corporate failures to three main factors viz. manipulation of financial statements, misuse of expense accounts and corruption at various levels. The best in few days back is ***B. Ramalinga Raju, Chairman; Satyam*** Computer Services has finally painted himself into a corner. Business today takes look at how the promoters of Satyam undid 21 years of endeavour in less than a fortnight. The six Satyam's deadly sins are as follows:

1. ***Proposing a selfish, high-risk acquisition:*** Mr. Raju announced to acquire two families owned businesses i.e. 100 per cent share holding in Maytas properties and 51% in Maytas infrastructure.
2. ***Overvaluing the proposed acquisition:*** Analyst consider dishonest is the price the cash-rich Satyam was willing to

pay for the two Maytas firms. Raju was willing to pay 6500 crore but net worth of the Maytas firms was 1125 crore.

3. ***Promoters pledging their entire holdings:*** The promoters informed Satyam that all their shares in the company were pledged with institutional lenders, and that some lenders may exercise or may have exercised their option to liquidate shares at their discretion to cover margin calls.
4. ***Refusing to resign:*** Nine days after Satyam announced its aborted acquisition bid, five Directors quit the Satyam. The big question, however, is should the management itself have resigned, given the huge breach of corporate governance at the company.
5. ***Not being able to utilize cash effectively:*** Satyam had cash of ₹5300 crore on its balance sheet, which it did not seem to be utilizing as effectively as some of its competitors were doing.
6. ***Messing up a sound company:*** It has some 690 clients and 28 development centers around the world, that's nothings to be sneezed at, it's a pity somebody did.

Corporate Governance: Worldwide

Corporate governance guidelines and best practices have evolved over a period of time. The Cadbury report, on financial aspects of corporate governance published in UK during 1992 was the starting point. Though the issues of corporate governance differ in each country depending on corporate traditions, tax laws and regulations, two broad types can be identified. The first is the case of US and Britain and the second type is found in Japan and Europe, notably in Germany. The two models reflect the different ownership patterns of companies.

The US approach to corporate governance has been to minimize conflicts of interest between owners and managers. This is attempted by giving mangers profit related incentives such as shares and stock options. Oversight by outside directors is sought to be sought to be strengthened by devices such as the audit and other committees that go into the details of the corporation's functioning.

In Germany there is statutory role the employees in the corporate governance system. The ownership of property is seen as imposing concomitant duties for its use for public weal. Unlike in USA, where banks connot trade in securities, banks in Germany not only provide long-term finance but also hold stocks of companies.

Today the corporate governance model in India is a mix of the US and Germany models. This is because of the way capital is raised here. Historically development agencies provided money for growth, however, in recent times a fairly active capital market has been doing this job. Corporate governance is regulated by SEBI enacting takeover code, depository act and introducing corporate governance clause 49 as a part of listing agreement. If we consider some recent happenings for example Escort transferred 4.73 million shares held in escort tractors to at book value and not market value, this lost 55.24 crore, ITC Bhadrachalam reportedly selling ITC finance and investment to ITC classic at a price of 23.8 crore which was lower 14 crore than its net value and Satyams' manipulation of accounts worth Rs.8000 crores.

After three unsuccessful attempts made in 1993, 1997 and 2003 to revise the companies Act 1956 the present UPA government has taken a fresh initiative once again and released a concept paper on company law in 2004. An expert committee under the chairmanship of Dr. JJ Irani was constituted on December 2004 to evaluate the comments an suggestions received on concept paper and provide recommendations to the government in making a simplified modern company law. The committee submitted its report on May 31, 2005. The contents of the committee report have been explained in 7 parts consisting of 13 chapters. Irani committee recommendations are relating to issues like board of directors (size, selection, age limit, tenure and remuneration etc), Relationships with stakeholders, audit and auditor, financial reporting and code of conduct.

Corporate Governance: Three Views

Corporate Governance issues are in general receiving greater attention as a result of the increasing recognition that a firm's corporate governance affects both its economic performance and its ability to access long term investment capital. We present below three different perspectives of governance.

i. ***J.J Irani,*** Director Tata Sons viewed that being ethical does not mean one cannot also profitable. It is most important to make profits and to generate wealth because only then can one have the resources to do good for the community. The differentiator between good and bad business practices is what happens to the wealth after it has been generated. He also viewed that we need a paradigm shift in our mindsets. Fortunately, mindsets are not permanent and these can be changed. We need to learn from our success stories rather than be bogged down by the tales of difficulty around us.

ii. ***Subir Raha,*** Chairman and MD, ONGC New Delhi viewed that corporate social responsibility, a jargon which we keep using very often, is not really a matter of giving away some money as charity or sponsoring or supporting some cause; it is actually the way corporates interact, the way they get involved with people outside, and, in the truest sense, their stakeholder some of whom happen to be their shareholders. When professional reach the top, they have to meet a lot of expectations from all the constituencies because when they become CEOs, by definition, the responsibility stops with them. And, this is where, to my mind, lies the essence of corporate governance. It is quite possible that managers will come to a point in their career where they know that if they stand up and disagree vocally, they will miss their next promotion or even lose their jobs. That would be the moment when they test their judgment on their learning or value system in terms of corporate governance.

iii. ***Suresh Prabhu,*** MP (Lok Sabha) opined that we have governments but not governance-that is the problem. And governments, by definition, do not provide governance. In the bureaucracy, governance is failing because nobody is responsible for delivering, nobody gets punishment for not delivering and nobody has any incentive for delivering.

Essential Governance Principles

The Basel Committee has issued several papers on specific topics. These include 'Framework for Internal Control Systems in Banking Organizations' (September-98) 'Enhancing bank Transparency' and Principles for the Management of Credit Risk (July-99).The following practices to avoid governance problems:

- The Company should lay solid foundations for management and oversight: recognize and publish the respective roles and responsibilities of board and management.
- Structure the board to add value: have a board of an effective composition, size and commitment to adequately discharge its responsibilities and duties.
- Actively promote ethical and responsible decision making.
- Safeguard integrity and financial reporting: have a structure to independently verify and safeguard the integrity of the company's financial reporting.
- Make timely and balanced disclosure of all material matters concerning the company.
- Respect the rights of the shareholders and facilitate the effective exercise of those rights.
- Recognize and manage risk through system of risk oversight and management and internal control.
- Fairly review and Encourage enhanced performance.
- Remunerate fairly and responsibly and its relationship to corporate and individual performance is defined.
- Recognize the legitimate interests of stakeholders.

- Corporate governance rating be made mandatory for listed companies.
- Ensure that the board members are well qualified and not subject to pressure.
- Ethical Approach: A clearly ethical basis to the business.
- Conducting corporate governance in a transparent manner.

Corporate Governance and Stakeholders Interests

namely, shareholders/Investors, employees, Customers, Suppliers and trading partners, community and environment.

Shareholders

The institutions see themselves as investors and not as owners. Their interest is in their funds and the performance of the funds rather than the companies in which they have invested. The small shareholder can claim very little moral influence as an individual in corporate performance.

Employees

It is clearly beneficial to the company to acquire, nourish and maintain a reputation for responsibility all round, including caring for the future of the employees. Fair treatment and active involvement of the workforce results in great benefits from loyalty to efficiency.

Customers

Frequent contact with all customers is needed to keep them from deserting, and the level of their satisfaction and happiness with the company has to be assessed periodically, and strengthened, and their perception of corporate governance must be respected.

Suppliers and Trading Partners

The old fashioned adversarial attitude has given place to partnership relationship with suppliers and dealers. It means working together for common good and mutual benefit. No one can deny its influence on their governance. This trend of products being purchased within the network of such partnerships is growing. Close customer-supplier relationships are developed resulting in such efficient processes as JIT (Just in Time)

Community and Environment

The impact on environment is highly influential not only for the present but also for the future. The environmental issues are highly ethical because they also are compounded with the issue of human rights of the affected.

The State

The corporations must be a good citizen. If the state demands a high rate of tax, the industry will seek defensive measures much against the interest of society. A balance needs to be struck which benefits all parties.

Approach to Good Corporate Governance

The law sets minimum standards of conduct. But it does not and cannot embody the whole duty of man, and mere compliance with the law does not necessarily good company. The following steps are recommendable for good governance.

1 ***Independent board:*** constitution of board with at least 50 per cent independent directors.

2 ***Employees' participation:*** For better governance, employees' participation and motivation, and given higher priority.

3 ***Operational performance:*** on the operational side, the companies have to implement risk management system for the whole company and periodical reporting and assurance to board be made on quarterly basis.

4 ***Disclosure:*** no doubt financial transparency and discipline is a must, but what is required is the fairness to all, compliance to law.

Conclusion

The separation of the owner and the manager in a modern public owned company has given rise to the concept of corporate governance. Liberalization and globalization have led to greater interest in the corporate governance practices in India. Lately a number of examples of corporate miss-governance have emerged which accentuate the need for better corporate governance in this country. In short, Corporate Governance is about commitment to values and ethical business conduct. The relationship of board and management with:

- Shareholders should be characterized by candor;
- Employees by fairness;
- Society by good citizenship; and
- Government by commitment to compliance.

Governance is based on organizational culture and leadership. It is a journey and not destination. A journey the route of which should be decided by the corporate. It is the journey never ending and a journey for the growth and value addition. The Corporate governance must address the issues of interplay between companies' shareholders, creditors, capital markets, financial sector institutions, and the state represented by Company Law. It is a fairly substantive and radical code. It is vital for the well-being of corporate India it is what makes a company into 'My Company'. Corporate governance abuses perpetrated by a dominant shareholder pose a difficult regulatory dilemma in that regulatory intervention would often imply a micro-management of routine business decisions. The regulator is forced to confine himself to broad proscriptions which leave little room for discretionary action. Many corporate governance problems are ill–suited to this style of regulation. In short, the key to better corporate governance in India today lies in a more efficient and vibrant capital market. Over a period of time, it is possible that Indian corporate structures may approach the Anglo-American pattern of near complete separation of management and ownership. At that stage, India too would have to grapple with governance issues like empowerment of the board. Until then, these issues which dominate the Anglo-American literature on corporate governance are of peripheral relevance to India.

References

Bhide and Amar "Efficient Market, Deficient Governance" *Harward Business Review,* November-December 1994 pp No. 128-139.

Bajaj, R., Chairman, (1997) *Draft Code on Corporate Governance*, Confederation of Indian Industry.

Balasubramaniam, N. (1997) "Towards Excellence in Board Performance", *The IIMB.Management Review*, January-March, 67-84.

Barua, S. K. and Varma, J. R. (1993a), "FERA in Reverse Gear; MNCs Strike Gold", *Economic Times*, November 12, 1993.

Barua, S. K. and Varma, J. R. (1993b), "MNCs Must be Subjected to SEBI Acquisition.Code", *Economic Times*, November 17, 1993.

Boyd Colin "Ethics and Corporate Governance: The Issues Raised by the Cadbury Report in the United Kingdom" *Journal of Business Ethics* Vol.15 Issue 2, February-1196 pp 167-182.

Corporate Governance in Public Sector Banks-Issue and Challenges by Ambika Prasadpati and Vijay Kumar, *Journal of Accounting and Finance* Vol. 19, No.1 October-2004 and March-2005.

Corporate Governance in the United Kingdom: The Rise of Fiduciary Capitalism- A Review of Literature by James P Hawley and Andrew T. Williams LENS inc's Internet Site.

Cadbury, A., Chairman, (1992), *Report on the Financial Aspects of Corporate Governance.*

Corporate Governance by H.Narayanan Retd. Chief (PR and Publicity) *Yogakshema* Vol.45, No.11 November-2001.

J.J Irani Committee Report on Company Law related to Corporate Governance by S.C Das *The Management Accountant*, September 2005.

Jones, Randall S.Tsuru, Kotaro "Japan Corporate Governance: A System in Evolution" OECD Observer, Issue 204, February-March 1997, pp 40-41.

New Dimensions in Global Business Perspective–2001 edited by B. Bhattacharyya Excel Book New-Delhi 1998.

Opening Address Delivered by J.J Irani, Subir Raha and Suresh Prabha on *'Corporate and Public Governance'* on November 29, 2005 during the conference held at IIM-Ahmedabad.

Productivity Promotion, Vol. 10 No. 36

The Working Group on Corporate Governance "A New Compact for Owners and Directors" *Harward Business Review* July-August 1991 pp 141-143.

3

Business Ethics and Corporate Social Responsibility

Dr. Hailay Gebretinsae
Dr. Aravind S.
Dr. Fisseha Girma Tessema

Abstract

Business ethics a subject that for years has been low profile in business publications and business shall curriculum, has suddenly gained status. The word ethics was once considered irrelevant by corporate loyalists, but now discussion of it is increasingly seen as not only important but also as critical to a company's success. Ethics refers to system of moral principles—a sense of right and wrong, and goodness and badness of actions and the motives and consequences of these actions. As applied to business firms, ethics is the study of good and evil, right and wrong, and just and unjust actions of businessmen.

The intensity of consumer movements and the rising level of awareness among corporate stakeholders are making it difficult for corporate to get away with unethical business practices. Now stakeholders and consumers are not longer indifferent to unethical practices like financial irregularities, tax-evasion, poor quality products and service, kick-backs, non-compliance within environmental issues, and hazardous working conditions. Indian corporates have lately realized that integrity, transparency, and open communications are the new norms of the corporate world. They also believe that the goodwill resulting from adopting a code of business ethics will in the long run, translate into economic gains in the form of stock market.

Key Words: Ethics, Corporate, Culture, Responsibility, Business, Governance etc.

Introduction

Business ethics a subject that for years has been low profile in business publications and business shall curriculum, has suddenly gained status. The word ethics was once considered irrelevant by corporate loyalists, but now discussion of it is increasingly seen as not only important but also as critical to a company's success.

Ethics refers to system of moral principles—a sense of right and wrong, and goodness and badness of actions and the motives and consequences of these actions. As applied to business firms, ethics is the study of good and evil, right and wrong, and just and unjust actions of businessmen.

Two Theories Are Pertinent When One Talks About The Nature of Ethics

The theory of Moral unity essentially advocates the principle that business actions should be judged by the general ethical standards of the society. There exists only one set of ethical standards which applies to business and non-business situations.

Theory of Amorality, which argues that business, can be amoral, and actions of businessmen need not be guided by general ethical standards. Managers may act selfishly because the market mechanism distils their actions into benefits to shareholders and the society at large.

Sources of Business Ethics

HR Manager in every society is influenced by three repositories of ethical values: Religion, Culture and Law

Religion

One of the oldest sources of ethical inspiration is religion. The principle of reciprocity towards one fellow human beings is found in all major religions. The great religions preach the necessity for an orderly social system and emphasize social responsibility with an objective to contribute to the general welfare.

Culture Experience

Culture refers to asset of values. Rules and standards transmitted among generations and are aimed at modelling behaviours so that they fall within acceptable limits. These rules and standards always play an important part in determining values, because individuals anchor their conduct in the culture of the group in which they belong.

The Legal System i.e. Law

Laws are rules of conduct, approved by legislature, that guide human behavior in any society. They codify ethical expectations and change as new evils emerge. Whatever ethics the law codifies, it is binding on businesses. The society expects businesses to abide by the law. Obeying the law is presumed to be ethical behaviour.

Why is Ethics Important?

- It is man's basic nature that he desires to be ethical; not only in his private life but also in his business affairs where, being a manager, he knows that his decisions may affect the lives of thousands of employees. The basic ethical needs compel the organizations to be ethically oriented
- Values create credibility with the public. A company perceived by the public to be ethically and socially responsive will be honored and respected even by those who have no intimate knowledge of its actual working.
- The HR management can have credibility with its employees simply because it has credibility with the public. Neither a sound business strategy, nor a generous compensation policy and fringe benefits can win employee credibility, but perceived moral and social uprightness can.
- Ethical attitude helps the management make better decisions, that is, decisions which are in the interest of the public, their employees and the company's own long-terms good, even though the decision making is slower.
- Ethics and Profit go together. Value-driven companies are most likely to be successful in the long run, though in the short run, they may lose money.

- Law cannot protect the society, ethics can. Ethics is important because the government, law and lawyers cannot do everything to protect the society. Where law fails, ethics can succeed. An ethically-oriented management takes measures to prevent pollution and protect workers' health even before being mandated by the the law. An ethically sound HR Manager, who can reach out to agitated employees, will quell a trouble more effectively than the police.

Below table shows the number of frauds in the financial sector in India. These scams reinforce the assertion that many Indian businessmen are unethical. But corruption is not peculiar to any country, it is universal as show in the table give below.

Financial Scams	
Major Financial Scams	Amount Involved (Rs. in Crore)
Securities Scam, 1992	7,720
Indian Bank,1997	838
Madhepura Cooperative Bank, 2001	137
UTI Scam (Cyberspace)	32
Mafcon Case,2001	50
Premier Vinyl Case	115

Source: Human Resource and Personnel Management, K. Aswathappa

Greasing the Palms

Ethical Dilemmas

Several ethical dilemmas confront an HR Manager. The ethical dilemmas arise from three sources they are face to face ethics, corporate politics ethics and functional area ethics

Face to face ethics: These arise mainly there is a human element in most business transactions. It is likely that the quality assurance and overlooks a miner defects and approves a lot deliver by a supplier because of the personal relationship that the two enjoy. It is also not unlikely that a supervisor overrates the performance of an employee because of the similar relationship that exists between two.

Are Business Ethical?:

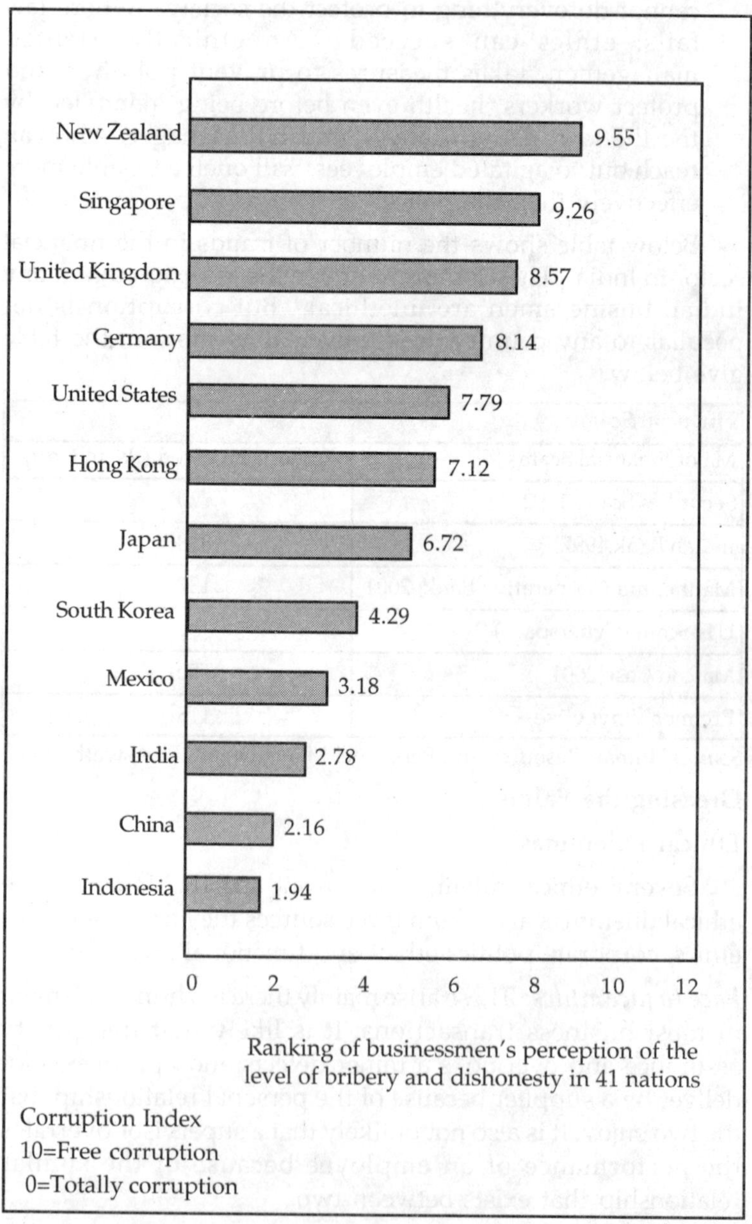

Corporate politics ethics: Companies are often faced with ethical dilemmas that affect their operations across all departments and divisions. Another issue relates to the consequences of employment contraction in labour intensive basic industries because of the improved methods of production. Modern technology has replaced older method of production which has in turn resulted in hundreds being rendered jobless.

The ethical burden of deciding corporate policy matters normally rest upon a company's HR management.

Functional area ethics: Accounting statements reveal to the manager and owners the financial soundness of the company. Manager, investors, regulating agencies, tax collectors and trade unions rely on accounting data to make decisions. Honesty, integrity and accuracy are absolute requirements of accounting functions. Professional accounting organizations generally accepted accounting standard (GAAPs) whose purpose is to establish uniform std for reporting accounting data. When they are followed these standards ensure high level of honest and ethical counting disclosures. Rarely are they followed in factories:

Ethical dilemmas croup up in purchasing departments where strong pressures are felt to obtained the lowest possible prices from suppliers and where suppliers too feel a similar need to bag lucrative contracts. Bribes kick backs, and discriminatory pricing or temptations to both the parties.

Marketing is another area of ethical issue. Pricing, promotions, Advertising, product information, relation between the ad agencies and their clients and marketing research have potential areas of ethical dilemmas.

Then there is a area of today's sophisticated communication technology which is grossly abused or misused to realize once ambitions.

HR Ethical issues

Ethical Issues Abound in HR Activities

Areas of ethical miss contact in the personal function

include employment remuneration and benefits, labour relations, health and safety and others.

Cash and Incentives Plan

These include base salaries, annual incentive plans, long term incentive plans, executive perquisites and separation agreements.

Base Salaries

The HR function is often presumed to justify a higher level of base salaries or higher percentage increase than what competitive practice call for. In some cases , pressure is exerted to re evaluate the position to a higher grade for the purpose of justifying a larger than normal increase.

Annual Incentive Plans

The HR manager is often foresee to design and administer top manager incentive plans, at higher rates than what the individuals deserve. A common rationale presented to the HR executive for bending the rules is the fear of losing the outstanding executives, if higher incentives are not paid.

Long Term Incentive Plan

Just as with annual incentive plan, many HR executives have the responsibility of designing and administering the firm's long term incentive plans, but in consultation with the CEO and an external consultant. Ethical issues arise when the HR executive is put to pressure to favor top management interests over those of other employees and investors.

Executive Perquisites

Executive perquisites make the ethical stand of the HR executive difficult because their cost is often out of proportion to the valve added. The responsibility of administrating these programmes falls on the HR executives who must live with the excesses that often are practiced. Excesses often sound bizarre, as for example, the transport of a CEO's pet German shepherd as the sole passenger, carried the manifest has 'G. Shepherd'. Another story related to a Bangalore based, loss-making public sector undertaking, whose CEO spent 20lakh to get a swimming pool built at his residence.

Performance Appraisal

Performance appraisal lends itself ethical issues. Assessment of the individual's is based on observation and judgement. HR managers are expected to observe the performance (or understands the potentials) in order to judge its effectiveness. Yet, some HR managers assign performance rating based on unrelated factors (for example, the employee is not loyal to the rater, or the rate belongs to a different caste or religion).

Ethics should be the corner stone of performance evaluations, and the overall objective of high ethical performance reviews should be to provide an honest assessment of the performance and mutually develop a plan to improve the ratiee's effectiveness.

Race, Gender, Age and Disability

The practice of treatment of employees according to their race, ethnic origin, sex, or disability has largely been stopped. A framework of loss and regulations has evolved that has significantly improved workspace behaviour. The threat of litigation and the attendant cost have spurred employers to introduce several programs design to train managers and supervisor to avoid discriminatory practices. No enterprise today would dare to publicly state that it denies minorities, women and the disabled opportunities for employment, remuneration, and growth prospects different from those given to others.

In this environment the role of HR function is to:

1. Monitor the principles and norms of the enterprise to ensure that they reflect the values of the society as express in its laws
2. Monitor the selection, reward, development, and appraisal system to ensure that they are consistence with the principles and norms
3. Vigorously pursue violations and, when necessary, vigorously work to defined the enterprise against unfounded allegations

A demanding ethical challenge arises when there is a pressure to protect the firm or an individual at the expense of someone else during an investigation

Employment Issues

While discrimination and harassment situations receive most publicity, HR practitioners are more likely to face ethical dilemmas in the areas of employee hiring. One challenge commonly encountered is pressure to hire a relative or a friend of a highly placed executive.

Another area related to employment is that of faked credentials submitted by a job applicant. While discovery of this kind of fabrication usually leads to termination of the employment, the choice becomes difficult when the applicant has a rare blend of skills-set and a proven tract record with his or her previous employers.

The challenge becomes more intense when it is discovered that an employee who has been with the firm for some time, a rare blend of skills-set has established a successful record, lied about his or her educational credentials.

Privacy Issues

Privacy refers to protecting a person's private life from intrusive and unwarranted actions. The employee believes that his or her religious, political and social beliefs as well as personal life-style are private matters and should be safeguarded from being snooped or analyzed. Exceptions are permitted grudgingly only when job involvement is clearly involved. For example, it may not be inappropriate to intrude into an employee's private matters if it is suspected that he or she discusses with a competitor, through e-mail messages, the specifications of a newly developed product not yet launched into the market.

Information Technology

A firm's need for information particularly about employees while-on- work may be at odds with the employees' privacy. There are regulations prohibiting third- party interception of e-mails without prior authorization, but interception by insiders is not covered by any law, and no absolute privacy exists in a computer based system. Employees are viewed on close-circuit TV, Phones are tapped, and computer files are read without his or her knowledge or consent. Such intrusions do breach the privacy of employees and constitute an ethical dilemma for the HR practitioner.

AIDS Testing

AIDS has become a major public health problem. Emerging first among homosexual males and drug users, the AIDS epidemic now affects all segments of the world population.

For the HR manager the disease raises two issues. Whether a new hire be subject to AIDS test? What treatment should be meted out to an employee who is affected with the disease? Opponents of AIDS testing argue that new hires should not be tested for the presence of HIUV because it would be an invasion of Privacy. They also argue that the available tests are frequently inaccurate and the tests do not reveal whether a person having AIDS antibodies will ever develop the disease.

Whistle Blowing

The third area of ethical concern for the HR manager relates to whistle-blowing. Like the blowing of a whistle by a referee to indicate violations of the rules on a playing field, whistle-blowing in a business setting refers to disclosure by former or current organization members of any illegal, immoral, or illegitimate practices involving their employers. Employees either make organizational misconduct public or inform it to top-level officials of the company.

How is Whistle-blowing an Ethical Issue?

Generally employees' area not expected to speak against their own employers because there is public interest in allowing firms to operate without harassment from insiders. Company information is generally considered to be proprietary and private. If employees, based on their personal points of view are freely allowed to expose issues to the public, the company may be thrown into turmoil and be unable to operate efficiently. On the other hand, there may be situations in which the society's interests override those of the company. So an employee may feel it obligatory to blow the whistle. The following sequence of actions morally justify whistle-blowing.

1 An unreported act that would be serious and would cause considerable harem to the people

2. Once such an act has been identified, the employee has reported the act to his or her immediate supervisor and has made the moral concern known.

3. If the immediate supervisor does nothing, the employee tries other internal pathways for reporting the problem

Genetic Testing

This testing is an attempt to use the science of genetics to understand the links between one's inherited characteristics and certain illnesses. Genetic testing can occur in two different forms: genetic screening and Genetic testing

Drug Testing

Pros and Cons of Employees Drug Testing
Arguments Favouring Employee Drug Testing
• Improves Employees productivity • Promotes safety in the workplace • Decreases employee theft and absenteeism • Reduces health and insurance costs
Arguments opposing employee Drug Testing
→ Invades an employee's privacy → Violates an employee's right to due process May be unrelated to job performance May be used as a method of employee discrimination Lowers Employee morale Conflicts with company values of honesty and trust May yield unreliable test results Ignores effects of prescription drugs, alcohol and over the counter- drugs Drug use is an insignificant problem for some companies

Genetic Screening

This is used to identify persons who are susceptible to certain genetically based illness. The goal of screening is to single out individuals or groups of people who have certain genetic traits.

Genetic Monitoring

This is used to identify substances that are capable of causing damage to the genetic make up of people. Genetic testing makes sense for business. Fewer disabled workers means reduction in costs caused by illness, absenteeism, health insurance, worker's compensation and turnover. Even today a boy with white patches on his skin will not get a girl in marriage and a girl with such blots finds it almost impossible to make a boy accept her in marriage.

Safety and Health

Modern business establishments are obviously full of hazards to safety and health. At the same time there is controversy surrounding the issues relating to safety and health. It may be asserted that nobody, including an employer, has a right to cause injury to the physique of another or damage his or her health. This assertion stems from the fact that health and safety are the two things that are highly valued. If anything can be said to be intrinsically good, it is health and safety. Except in the most extreme circumstances, life is better than death, health is better than illness and body integrity is better than injury. Besides this intrinsic value, health and safety also have significant instrumental value.. In other words, they are very useful for acquiring other things of value. Whatever one desires, being healthy and safe will improve one's chances for satisfying that desire. Thus safety and health have both intrinsic as well as instrumental value.

Restructuring and Layoffs

There are ethical implications in the process by which termination decisions are made and actions taken. For example, if restructuring requires closing of a plant, the process by which that plant is chosen, how the news will be communicated, and the time-frame for completing the lay-offs are ethically important. If conducted in an atmosphere of fairness and equity and with the dignity of the affected individuals in mind, the action is ethical. To start with, alternatives to lay-off may be tried before terminating services of employees. Following are the straightforward choices:

- Proportionally reducing work hours to spread the pain of reduced employment costs across the entire work-force.
- Reducing wages for all employees to reduce the wage bill
- Taking work previously outsourced
- Building inventory when demand is slack
- Freezing hiring to avoid making overstaffing worse
- Having people do other things, such as defer maintenance and repair, training courses and similar activities for which they were too busy when business was better
- Refraining from hiring to meet peak demand, which makes reductions in employment almost inevitable when demand falls.
- Encouraging people to develop new products, services, or markets so that their skills can still be used by the firms
- Putting production or staff people into sales to build demand

Means to promote Ethical Conduct

Empolyee Responsibilites	India	Asia Pacific	Global
Ethics/Code of Conduct	72	73	64
Pre-Employment Screening	54	37	50
Public Source Information	32	25	33
Whistle blowing System	28	18	28
Fraud Training	24	25	29
Others	23	20	27

Employees owe responsibilities to themselves and their own moral integrity, to their families, to their profession, to the law and to society at large. Obviously, employees face many cases of conflicting responsibilities in the workplace, as for instance, responsibility to one's employer versus obligation to public safety, or responsibility to one's profession is lore sacred than loyalty to the employer. The issue relating to self versus employer is Nothing but work-life balancing, an issues that is assuming increasing importance these days.

Managing Ethic

In the past, it was assumed in most firms that ethics was a matter of individual conscience. But the scenario has changed. Today, many businesses are using managerial interventions to ensure ethical conduct is worth stating in this context.

Code of Conduct in Tata

For the Company	*For the Employees*
To supply good and services of the highest quality standards to ensure total satisfaction of customers	Conduct themselves prfessional with honesty, integrity, as well as high moral and ethical standards. to be fair transparent and to be seen so by third parties
To engage only in activities beneficial to the national interest of the country they operate in	Not derive any benefit from any information about the company or group which constitutes inside information
To be fully transparent in accounting and financial reporting standards	Report to the management any actual or possible violation of the code or an event that the employee becomes aware of, that could affect the business or reputation of the employee's company or any other company belonging to the Tata group
To fully stic for the establishment and support of a competitive open-market economy and to abhor unfair trade practices	Permits employees to pursue an active role in civic or political affairs as long it does not affect interests the business or of the company or the group

(Contd...)

To neither give nor take any illegal payment, remuneration, gift, donation, or comparable benefit to obtain business or favours	—
To comply with all regulations regarding preservation of the environment	—
To be a good corporate citizen and to actively assist in the improvement of the life of the community with the objective of making it self-reliant	—
These social activities are regarded as an integral part of their business plans and not optimal	
To co-operate and share physical, human and management resources with other companies belonging to the Tata group so long as this does not adversely affects its business interests and shareholder value	—

Ethics Committees

Many companies have ethics committees to advice on ethical issues. Such a committee can be a high level on compromising the Board of Directors, Chaired by the CEO of the company.

The committees' field questions from employees help the company in establishing policies in new or uncertain areas, advise the board of directors on ethical issues, and oversee the enforcement of the code of Ethics.

Ethics Hotline

In some Companies, when Employees are troubled about some ethical issue but may be reluctant to raise it with their immediate supervisor, they can call on the company's 'Ethics Hotline'. A member of the ethics committee receives the confidential call and then quickly investigates the situation. Elaborate steps are taken to protect the identity of the caller, so as to encourage more employees to report any such deviant behaviour. This technique is advantageous in as much as the matter is settled internally, which is better for a company than to have a situation where disgruntled employees take their ethical complaints to the media.

Whistle Blowing

When an Employee thinks that his or her firm is resorting to some act that is unethical or harmful to public, he or she 'blows the whistle' by reporting alleged organizational misconduct to the public or to top executives. Whistle Blowing refrains the firm from indulging in unethical and harmful practices.

Ethics Training Programmes

Nearly all companies, which take ethics seriously, provide training in ethics to their managers and other employees. In such training programmes, company personnel are made familiar with the official Company policy on ethical issue, and it is shown how those policies can be translated into the specific everyday decision making.

Corporate Culture and Ethical Climate

Corporate culture is a blend of ideas; customs, traditional practices, company values, and shared meanings that help define normal behavior for everyone who works in a company. Every Organization has a culture which exercises considerable influence on employee behaviour.

Hewlett-Packard is well known for a culture that stresses on values and ethics. Call the 'HP'way' by employees, the modest important values of the culture are confidence in and respect for people, open communication, sharing of benefits and responsibilities, concern for the individual employees, and honesty and integrity.

Improving Ethical Decision Making

Ethical decisions are difficult to make. They cannot be programmed like Production and Inventory decisions.

The Components of Ethical Climate

		Focus of Ethical Concern	
Ethical Criteria	Individual	Company	Society
Egoism (Self-centered approach)	Self-interest	Company Interest	Economic Effciency
Benevolence (Concerns) for others) apporach	Friendship	Team Interest	Social Responsibility
Principle (Integrating approach	Personal Morality	Company rules and procedures	Laws and prfessional codes

Difficulties in Decision Making

- Managers face dilemmas in decision-making on a course of action.
- Managers confront situations where a distinction between facts and values has to be made while making ethical decisions.
- The good and evil exist simultaneously, in tandem, and are inter-related. Nestlé's sales of infant formula in Kenya and Zambia have led to infant deaths as mothers mixed the powdered food with contaminated local water and their babies died of dysentery. But evidence also shows that the same formula has saved other infants. Evils should be minimized if not eliminated.
- Antagonistic interests frequently use incompatible ethical arguments to justify their intentions. Eg: Animal Lovers may argue against slaughter on the ground that animals are entitled to rights similar to those enjoyed by humans, including the right to live. Poultry growers, on the other hand, contend that raising animals for food ensures benefits to society.
- Some Ethical standards vary with the passage of time.

Donations to political parties were forbidden earlier, but it is allowed now. In addition, certain bribes and payments are practiced in the Asian, African, and Latin American countries but are not regarded as ethical in the US. Doing business with close friends and family is a standard practice in the Arab world, but is treated as nepotism in Western Europe.

- Ethical Behaviour is moulded from the clay of human imperfection. Unethical practices abound everywhere. An honest HR manager finds himself or herself like a babe in the woods, not able to do anything, surround as he or she is by dishonesty everywhere.
- The growth of large scale organizations in the 21st century gives new significance to ethical problems such as committee decision-making that masks individual responsibility, organizational loyalty versus loyalty to the public interest, and preferential hiring of disadvantaged sections of society.

Ways of Resolving Ethical Issues

The individual in business can take number of steps to resolve ethical problems;

1. ***Moral Idealism:*** This postulates that certain acts are good and others asre bad. Pursue those acts which are good and avoid the bad ones. Moral idealism gives definite answer to ethical issues
2. ***Intuition:*** This leaves it to the individual HR Practitioner to sense the moral gravity of the situation. If he or she feels that his or her motives are good and that they do not intend to hurt anyone, he or she is taking an intuitive approach to morally difficult situations
3. ***Utilitarianism:*** This seeks to establish the moral locus not on the act or the motives but on the consequences. If the consequences represent a net increase in the society's happiness, or at least not a decrease, the act is morally right.

Corporate Social Responsibility

Classification of stakeholders

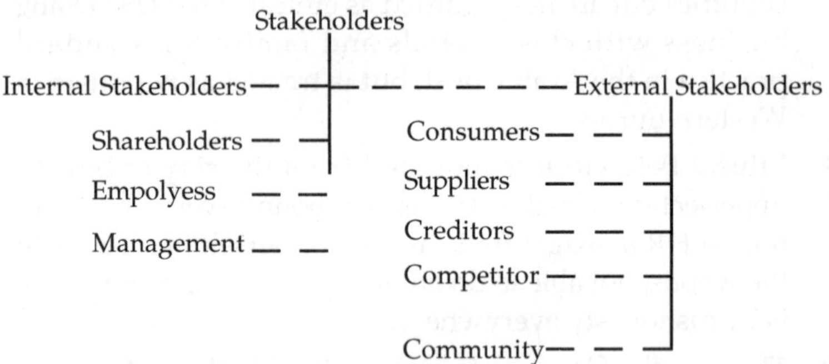

Internal Stakeholders

Shareholders Responsibilities

- Maintaining good relationships with top management
- Exercising their voting rights

Similarly, the organization must honour the trust of the shareholders. Therefore the responsibilities of the organization towards the shareholders are:

- Managing the company efficiently in order to secure a fair and competitive return on the owner's investment
- Disclosing relevant information to shareholders, subject only to legal requirements and competitive constraints
- Conserving, protecting, and increasing the shareholder's assets
- Respecting the shareholders requests, suggestions, complaints and formal resolutions.

Employees

Responsibilities of Employees and Employers

Some specific Responsibilities of organization towards their employers are:

- To provide adequate compensation

- To provide working conditions that respect each employee's health and dignity
- To be honest in communications with employees and open in sharing information
- To listen to and where possible, act on employee suggestion, ideas, requests and complaints
- To engage in negotiations when conflict arises
- To avoid discriminatory practices and guarantee equal treatment and opportunity regardless of gender, age, race and religion
- To protect employees from avoidable injury and illness in the workplace
- To encourage and assist employees in developing skills and knowledge that are required to for accomplishing the task

McDonald's—Commitment of Employees

Our People Promise is more than words. McDonald's and its independent owners or operators have made a commitment to employees that we strive to achieve with our actions every day. These people principles reflect McDonald' values describe the culture we embrace

Respect and Recognition

Managers treat employees as they would want to be treated Employees are respected and valued Employees are recognized formally for good work performance, extra effort, and teamwork and customer service.

Values and Leadership Behaviours

All of us act in the best interest of the company

We communicate openly, listening for understanding and valuing diverse opinions

We accept personal accountability

We coach and learn Competitive pay and Benefits

(Contd...)

Pay is at or above local market rates
Employees value their pay and benefits
Learning, Development and Personal Growth
Employees receives work experience that teaches skills and values that last a lifetime
Employees are provided the tools they need to develop personally and professionally
Resources to get the job done
Employees have the resources they need to serve the customer
Restaurants are adequately staffed to allow for a good customer experience as well s to provide schedule flexibility, work-life balance and time for training

Source: www.mcdonalds.com

Management

According to stakeholder theory an organization should not give preferential treatment to any stakeholder group over other. Therefore the task of the management is to keep the relationships among the stakeholders in balance. When these relationships become imbalanced, the survival of the firm is in jeopardy.

External Stakeholders

How Canadian Executives Describe Reputation of Management The conference Board survey asked respondents to rank four statements in order of how accurately they described their organization's approach to reputation management	
Statement	*Percentage*
Build strong shareholder relationship	54
Manage corporate and brand identity	25
Directly manage impression	13
Manage relationships with opinion Leaders	8

Consumers

The responsibilities fo business corporations towards their consumers are summed up by the five R's – the right quality, right quantity, right time, right place and right price. A few of these responsibilities are:

- Producing goods according to the specific needs of consumers, their purchasing power etc.
- Offering quality goods at reasonable prices
- Providing prompt and adequate service to consumers
- Improving the standard of living by producing goods and services of high quality
- Treating customers fairly in all aspects of business transactions
- Ensuring the health and safety of customers

Suppliers

A company's relationship with suppliers and sub contractors must be based on mutual respect:

- Seek fairness and truthfulness in all activities, including pricing and licensing
- Ensure that business activities are free from coercion and unnecessary litigation
- Foster long-term stability in the supplier relationship in return for value, quality,
- competitiveness and reliability
- Share the information with suppliers and integrate them in the planning processes
- Pay suppliers on time and in accordance with agreed terms of trade; and
- Seek, encourage and prefer suppliers and subcontractors whose employment practices respect human dignity

Creditors

Creditors play an important role in organizations. Usually organizations buy goods on credit from suppliers. Although suppliers have stake in a business, they may cease to fill orders if a company is unable to pay the amount due, or tasks too long in making the payment. Organizations often delay in repaying the credit to the creditors. The firm should consider the problem from both debtors and creditors view. Here, creditors are the suppliers who supply goods to the debtor or company as demanded. And the debtor, though is in position to pay, chooses the last possible moment. It is the responsibility of the organization to make timely payments for goods that have already been delivered.

Competitors

The responsibilities of the organization towards the competitors are;

- Foster open markets for trade and investment
- Promote competitive behaviour that si socially and environmentally beneficial and demonstrates mutual respect among competitors
- Refrain from either seeking or participating in questionable payments or favors to secure competitive advantage
- Respect both tangible and intellectual property rights
- Refuse to acquire commercial information by dishonest or unethical means such as industrial espionage

Community

A firm's responsibility towards the society includes:

- Respecting human rights and democratic institutions
- Supporting public policies and practices that promote human development through harmonious relations between business and other segments of society
- Collaborating with such activities that aim at improving

the standards of health, education, workplace safety and economic well-being

- Promoting and stimulating sustainable development and playing a leading role in preserving and enhancing the physical environment and conserving the earth's resources
- Supporting peace, security, diversity and social integration, respecting the integrity of local cultures
- Encouraging charitable donations, educational and cultural contributions and employee participation in community and civic affairs

Dabur—Social Responsibility

What is that life worth which cannot bring comfort to others, these word of Dr. S.K Burman have inspired generation of Dabur. Keeping these golden world in mind, Sundesh or the the sustainable development society was set up to carry out welfare activities aimed ata improving the quality of life of the rural people in its area of operation. This society is given compete financial and managerial support by Dabur India Limited Sundesh is engaged in providing health services, non-formal education and training in income generating activities. The society has a dedicated them consisting of a doctor, a community organizer, a lady social worker, and instructors for income generating activities. Sundesh organizes regular OPDs and health campus in the villages.

In addition to the mobile OPDs, other health services rendered include training or traditional birth attendants, immunization programs for children ,maintenance fo family health records, ante-natal checkups, pulse polio programmes and health awareness meeting for women to topics such as family planning, ante-natal care, post-natal care, the importance of vaccinations, baby-care and AIDS prevention.

Conclusion

Business can succeed only if they maintain good relationships with all their stakeholders. These relationships can be strengthened, if organizations fulfill their obligations towards stakeholders. According to late Prime Minister Lal Bahadur Shastri, 'Too often the community views the businessmen's aims as selfish gain rather than advancement of the general welfare. That impression can be removed only if business is fully alive to its social responsibilities and helps our society to function in harmony as one organic whole.

The intensity of consumer movements and the rising level of awareness among corporate stakeholders are making it difficult for corporate to get away with unethical business practices. Now stakeholders and consumers are not longer indifferent to unethical practices like financial irregularities, tax-evasion, poor quality products and service, kick-backs, non-compliance within environmental issues, and hazardous working conditions. Indian corporates have lately realized that integrity, transparency, and open communications are the new norms of the corporate world. They also believe that the goodwill resulting from adopting a code of business ethics will in the long run, translate into economic gains in the form of stock market.

References

Business Ethic and Corporate Governance, ICFAI Material

en.wikipedia.org

Human Resource and Personnel Management, K.Aswathappa

www.business-ethics.com

www.managementhelp.org

www.business-ethics.org

4

Corporate Social Responsibility
A Right Approach to Sustainable Business

Dr. Sudhansu Kumar Das

Abstract

In a global economy, increasingly organizations have a responsibility to facilitate, demonstrate and promote corporate social responsibility (CSR). Long-term sustainability demands that organizations rethink their business goals and objectives from solely focusing on making a profit to corporate citizenship. Today, the impact of CSR is beginning to be seen in communities throughout the world—from human rights and labour practices to healthcare and the environment. At home and abroad, HR plays a critical role—that of leading and educating their firms regarding the importance of CSR while at the same time strategically implementing sound HR management practices that support the company's business and CSR goals.

Introduction

India's economic growth over the last 15 years has provided an experience and expectation that the country could emerge as the third largest economy of the world in less than two decades by improving the standard of living of its one billion plus population. There has been a significant change in the structure of the Indian economy from agrarian economy to industrial economy and again to services sector economy today, as services sector is the prime mover of the economic growth (about 50 per cent of the GDP). With rise in the flow of FDI in to the country and boost in the consumption in the domestic as well as in overseas markets, the industrial sector of the country has registered a phenomenon rise in all key indicators viz. profits, employment, growth and investment. Moreover, Corporate India is fast becoming global as all major Indian enterprises have made their presence in all major destinations over the globe through the mechanism of acquisition and merger making the Indian business tycoons among the top billionaires of the world.

According to Frobes Report of the US Business Magazine, out of the total 500 top billionaires of the world, India alone accounts for 53 in numbers with combined wealth of $1.6 trillion, more than that of China (42 billionaires with $956 billions). The total wealth of Indian billionaires is $340.9 billion which is 31 per cent of the country's GDP. Indian billionaires accounts for 8 per cent of the world's billionaires and they got three times more weight than their US counterparts and 10 times than China. Against this, the country is having a big proportion of the people of the country (about 1/4th living below poverty line) are officially poor. Despite a respectable growth of our economy (about 8 per cent), inequalities in the standard of living between persons, regions and states have persisted and accentuated. The much talked and debated economic liberalization have brought growth opportunities for an insignificant proportion of the rich people living at the top of the social pyramid. Our hon'ble Prime minister has rightly quoted that liberalization has not benefited the poor people of the country and much is needed to improve in the social sector developments including education, health and poverty alleviation.

The UNDP statistical update 2008 places India at 132nd position (with HDI value of 0.609 in 2006) amongst 179 nations of the world. The poor ranking of GDP show how India is performing miserably in all key indicators including GDP per-capita, life expediency at birth, education at measured by adult literacy and gross enrolment rate. India's HDI rank at 132 is lower than its per capita GDP rank of 126, primarily because of low ranking on education and health.

Global Hunger Index 2007 of the International Food Policy Research Institute, Washington, ranks India 66 among 88 developing and transforming nations of the world, It is a established fact that the ongoing economic growth has benefited the people below poverty line than the ultra poor.Table—4.1 shows India's stand on HDI among major nations of the world.

Table—4.1 India's Global Position on Human Development, 2008

Country	HDI Index	GDP Per-capita (US $ PPP)	Life Expectancy at birth (Yr)	Adult Literacy Rate (% aged 15 yrs & above	Combined Gross Enrolment in Education (%)
Brazil	0.807 (70)	8,949 (77)	72.0 (81)	89.6 (98)	87.2 (39)
Russia	0.807 (73)	13,205 (55)	65.2 (12)	99.5 (12)	81.9 (49)
Thailand	0.786 (81)	7613 (80)	70.0 (102)	93.9 (75)	78.0 (68)
China	0.762 (94)	4682 (104)	72.7 (71)	93.0 (81)	68.7 (113)
Srilanka	0.742(104)	3896 (115)	71.9 (83)	90.8 (91)	68.7 (114)
Indonesia	0.726(109)	3455 (121)	70.1 (101)	91.0 (90)	68.0 (116)
India	0.609(132)	2489 (126)	64. (129)	65.2(148)	61.0 (134)

Source: UNDP Statistical Update 2008.

Keeping the poor social sector developments in the country, this papers is a sincere attempt to access the corporate social responsibility of the business with special emphasis to Indian corporate sector.

CSR- What Does it Mean?

CSR is increasingly a misunderstood and much debated concept worldwide. There is a saying in the business, "Business of the business is to do business and nothing else". Profit is the only and dominating objective of the business as profit is needed both for the working and growth of the business. However, CSR in fact becoming an increasing business strategy both nationally and globally. As globalization accelerates and large corporations serve as global providers, the CEOs and top executives over the globe have realized the role of CSR for sustainable business growth.

Corporate Social Responsibility has two broad concepts. The first is related to the shareholders. The company must adopt fair and good business practices to maximize the value of the business to the shareholders. The other concept is related to the society. From the social perspective, company must recognize the responsibility towards the social and environmental issues. CSR may be recognized as a strategic business practice and operating the business in such a manner that, the commercial, legal, ethical, social and public expectations are achieved. CSR is taken to mean sustaining economic activity by integrating social responsibilities of the enterprises in their external and internal relation with business prospects. It is thus, a comprehensive set of policies, practices and programmes that are integrative part of the business operations or activities aim at attaining social goals and addressing social causes.

The term CSR has been used interchangeably as Corporate Citizenship, Responsible Business, Sustainable Responsible Business, Corporate Social Performance and linked to the concept of Triple Bottom Line Reporting(TBR), which is used as a framework for measuring an organizational performance against economic, social, ethical and environmental parameters.

The rationale behind CSR is building sustainable business that requires their performance in all key areas. The Key drivers of CSR are as follow:

1. *Enlightened Self-interest:* Building a synergy of ethics, a cohesive society and sustainable global economy.
2. *Social Investment:* Contributing to social and physical infrastructure and social capital.
3. *Transparency and Trust:* More open, trustworthy, accountable business practices.
4. *Increased Public Expectation of Business:* To contribute more than providing employment and growth.

CSR—Few Definitions

"CSR is about how companies manage the business processes to provide an overall positive impact on society".

—Mallem Baker

"CSR is the continuing commitment by business to behave ethically and contribute to economic development while improving the quality of life of the workforce and their families as well as of the local community and the society at large".

—Lord Holme and Richard Watts

CSR is about capacity building for sustainable livelihoods. It represnts cultural differences and funds the business opportunities in building the skills of the employees, the community and the government".

—Ghana

"CSR is about business giving back to the society".

—Philippines

"Operating business in a manner that meets or exceeds the ethical, legal, commercial and public expectations that society has to business"

"A concept where by companies decide voluntarily to contribute to a better society and a cleaner environment. A concept where by companies integrate social and environmental concerns in their business operations and in their interaction with their stake holders on a voluntary basis".

European Commission

CSR in the Business Community

Worldwide, companies and their HR leadership are coming to grips with what exactly CSR means in their organizations and how to strategically include CSR within business goals and objectives. There is growing evidence pointing to the validity of and the demand for CSR. For example, 82 per cent of companies noted that good corporate citizenship helps the bottom line and 74 per cent said the public has the right to expect good corporate citizenship.

As the concept of CSR becomes more widely accepted and integrated in business, it is helpful in this discussion to understand that the development of CSR in organizations is in transition . There are basically three 'generations' of CSR in varying stages of sophistication. The first generation has demonstrated that companies can contribute to society without risking commercial success. Today, the second generation is developing more fully as CSR gradually becomes an integral part of companies' long-term business strategies. Finally, the third generation addresses significant societal issues, such as poverty and cleanup of the environment.

Corporations Should Only Aim for Profit?

Ardent supporters of free markets, such as Milton Friedman, have long argued that companies should not be diverted from their pursuit of profit; it ultimately harms a free society if entities such as companies try to act for a wider good other than its own self-interest, because it is hard to know what the wider good is, and damages the primary goal of companies: responsibility to shareholders.

In his book, *Capitalism and Freedom,* Friedman argues that "there is one and only one social responsibility of business—to use its resources and engage in activities designed to increase its profits so long as it stays within the rules of the game, which is to say, engages in open and free competition without deception or fraud"

His theories are appealing, though unfortunately in the real world, many companies, larger ones in particular are often involved in exploitative practices of some sort, knowingly or unknowingly (through sub-contractors, for example). Furthermore, with their increasing financial muscle comes increasing financial power in the political arena to influence policies in their favor. This is not necessarily engaging in open and free competition (some lobbying is often to actively prevent competition, for example).

Given the immense impact businesses can have on people's lives, and their increasing power, environmental, human-rights, and social justice activists have tried different ways to get businesses to be more accountable for their actions. They have tried to go through their government (that is supposed to be representative of their people, in a democracy), and even to businesses and shareholders themselves to urge better responsibility.

As a result, many business leaders have therefore tried to pursue corporate social responsibility practices or attempt to implement CSR in their organization.

Bad CSR is Bad Publicity

Companies that appear to be socially responsible by promulgating environment saving or environmental sustainability and, at the same time, being allegedly tangled in an illegal socially irresponsible activity is a tremendous message to send out to the stakeholders including consumers and investors. The effect of such CSR scandals is that credibility and the reputation of the company are undoubtedly badly damaged. There is an old saying that any publicity is good publicity. However, in the world of business, bad publicity is bad publicity, and can cost a company up to millions of dollars, with nothing to speak for goodwill. Corporate social responsibility articles in the news are often quick to fault wrong-doers.

CSR: A Milestone

1801 : Robert Owen's Cotton Mills, Scotland adopted the no child labour and workers Benefit Fund.

1892 : Jamsedji Tata set up the J.N. Endowment Scheme.

1913-15 : Henry Ford's double the wages scheme.

2000 : Bill Gate and wife Milanda constituted the Gates foundation.

CSR Model: Creative Capitalism *vs.* Social Business

Capitalism has revolutionized the way of life of the billions in the globe in one way or other. However, capitalism today misses out many important issues of human life including poverty, health, nutrition, housing etc. Realizing the urgent need for a structural change in the traditional capitalism, Bill Gate, the iconic hero of modern capitalism has advocated for a new and distinct theory called creative capitalism.

According to him, corporations have the skill to make technological innovations that can work for the benefit of the poor. To make these developments we need a more creative capitalism. It is san attempt to stretch the reach of the market forces so that more companies can benefit from doing work that can makes more people better off. We need new ways to bring for more people into the system of capitalism. Take the case of ICT, how they have brought significant change in our life including e-governance, tele-medicine, e-money, e-commerce, e-marketing, etc. Thus, creative capitalism is an answer to many vital issues. Creative capitalism can most effectively spread the benefits of capitalism and bring improvement in the standard of living of the poorer of the poor.

Prof. Md. Yonus, the father of microfinance has viewed in differently. He has advocated for social business to address the problems of the poor. His architructure of Social enterprise is a non-loss, non-dividend business with social gain. Instead of being profit driven, this will be cause driven. It will make profit. But, profit will not go to the investors, except getting back the investment money. His concept of social business has two business markets; both will go side by side. When social business identifies an opportunity for a profitable venture, it will draw huge investment and return.

CSR: Key Issues

A study by on CSR Asia has identified the following top ten issues for the future:

1. The Environment and Climate Change
2. Labour Rights as Human Rights
3. Transparency and Accountability
4. The Institutional of CSR

5. Stakeholders Engagement
6. The Battle for Talent
7. Community Investment
8. Supply Chain and Product Safety
9. Social Enterprises
10. Poverty Alleviation

CSR and Corporate India

CSR is a global phenomenon and Corporate India is not an exception to it. Corporate India is all set to improve the public image of the business. Social responsiveness is not a new concept for the Indian industries. However, response is encouraging as the companies presently recognizing the need of their social and environmental commitments and CSR has become a part of business strategy. Corporate Social Responsibility for the Indian companies is no more a philanthropy, rather imperative for successful business. Indian companies are spending 5 per cent of their profits for CSR activities.

Commitment of the Indian companies towards the social and environmental issues is a part of comprehensive awareness of the corporate world. In 1999, Kofi Annan, the then Secretary General of United Nations invited the global corporate leaders for global compact to promote nine principles covering three broad areas viz. human rights, labour rights and sustainable development. Several state-owned companies of India joined together to form Global Compact Society of India. In 2001, European and Indian Network for CSR was launched to bring together European and Indian companies and their stakeholders to address the major CSR issues. In 2004-05, United Nations Development Programmes(UNDP) and Confederation of Indian Industries(CII) in collaboration with the academic institutions have brought about 18 case studies of CSR ranging from NABARD to Times of India. It would be useful to highlight in brief the Social commitments of few Indian companies.

NABARD

- Empowerment of Rural women through micro-credit and micro enterprise programmes.
- Joint Liability Group and Rythu Mitra Sanghas for providing credit access to landless farmers, agriculture workers and oral lessees.
- Natural Resources Management initiatives for sustainable development of poor and the tribal.
- Financing supply chain management in agricultural produce market.
- Creation of special funds like Watershed Development Fund, Tribal Development Fund, Research Development Fund etc.
- Provision for large-scale employment through initiatives like Cluster Development, Rural Hats, Rural Industrial Programmes, Rural EDPs ect.

HPCL

- Supporting initiatives during natural calamities and emergencies.
- Improving the standard of living of the weaker section of the societies including the children, women and physically challenged.
- Focus on primary education, health, portable water, and sanitation.
- HIV/AIDs awareness programmes, empowerment of the youths and girls.

BPCL

- *Infrastructure Development:* Provision for tube wells, dug wells for drinking water and irrigation, construction of multi-purpose community center, school and health centre, etc.
- *Educational Support:* Provision for uniform, note books, educational aids, stationeries, nutritious food, scholarship for the poor students ect.

- *Health Care:* Provision for health check-up, free medicine, family welfare, AIDs/HIV prevention, cataract surgery etc.
- *Skill Development:* Adult education, modern farming practices, vocational training etc.

ONGC

- Support to schools, colleges, technical and scientific institutions etc.
- Aids and relief to rural poor, hospitals and clinics.
- Promoting agriculture, horticulture, dairy farming etc.
- Family welfare, healthcare and cluster development.
- Welfare and upliftment or rural communities.
- Industrial and vocational training.

NTPC

- *Education:* Supporting primary education, rural culture, aid to educational institutions, scholarships etc.
- *Health:* Health camps, associating and sponsoring national health programmes like T.B, AIDs, Polio etc.
- Power generation to villages
- Upliftment of neglected sections of the society
- Supporting programmes during natural calamities

CSR as Business Plan

Expenditures on CSR are no more treated as costs to the business, rather than creative investments. CSR initiatives are increasingly become the part of business strategies to achieve economic goals. Investment in fair and healthy CSR initiatives leads to increase in the image of the company as well as of the brand, getting public support, building sound industrial relation and reducing operating costs. Moreover, information on environmental and social impacts minimizes the degree of risks of the business. Corporate leaders today think that companies can create potential markets by helping the poor and corporate philanthropy is cost effective. A good number of business houses contribute voluntarily at their own initiatives to the social causes. Pepsi Co, the largest multinational soft-drinks co. as part of its CSR initiative has taken the task of fighting with HIV/AIDs. In collaboration with Bhoruka Public Welfare Trust (BPWT), it has stated the programme in Kolkata to spread awareness on HIV/AIDs and to popularize the use of condoms. According to the Company's senior executives, this programme will benefit the company to protect the young people of the age group between 18 and 35 who are more vulnerable to AIDs.

So far as CSR initiatives in the banking sector is concerned, Reserve Bank of India has given direction to undertake and promote sustainable development. Also the banks are asked to give non-financial reporting to give account of the bank's intangible assets.

Conclusion

To conclude, CSR does not mean philanthropy. It is a healthy and effective trade practice and good business plan. CSR is a Process that makes the business people aware of the impact of their works in the internal and external communities, environmental and outside world. CSR is a useful tool helping the Government to enforce labour, industrial and environmental laws. However, the CSR initiatives are at their infancy. Studies show that many Asian countries do not have awareness on global warming and climatic changes and their impact on economic activities. Corporate houses must develop broad and comprehensive plans to ensure sustainable developments. At the same time, Government at national, international and local level must make legal provisions to counteract the social and environmental impacts of the business and making the business houses responsible corporate citizens.

References

Business and Economy, Various Issues.

Business Standard, Various Issues.

CSR, *ASOCIO Policy* Paper 2004.

CSR ASIA. The Future for the Next Decades: Top 10 Issues.

file:/H:\Definitions of Corporate Social Responsibility.htm.

file:/H:\ISO 26000 (CSR Guidelines).htm

Venkata Raman, C.V., 'Service with Smile', *Economics Times,* April 28, 2006.

Venkata Ratnam S., *'CSR For Sustainable Development'*, Economics Times, April 28, 2006.

www.nabard.org.com.

5

Current Issues In Corporate Governance

Reasons for Corporate Governance Failures

Jagdish. R. Raiyani

Abstract

Corporate governance *is the set of processes, customs, policies, laws, and institutions affecting the way a corporation is directed, administered or controlled. Corporate governance also includes the relationships among the many stakeholders involved and the goals for which the corporation is governed. The principal stakeholders are the shareholders, management, and the board of directors. Other stakeholders include labour (employees), customers, creditors (e.g., banks, bond holders), suppliers, regulators, and the community at large.*

This chapter reveals various reasons for failure of Corporate Governance, Corporate Governance conists of various examples of Corporate Governance failures like Enron, Satyam, Cadbury, Wal-Mart, Xerox and why Corporate Governance failed in such big organizations. paper also describes various mechanisms of Corporate Governance like (1) Company's Act (2) Security law (3) Discipline of capital market (4) Nominees on company board (5) Statutory audit (6) Codes of conduct etc. Some factors that influence the Corporate Governance like Owernership structure, Structure of company board, Financial structure, Institutional Environment etc. Various systematic problem in Corporate Governance and Recent Corporate Governance failures.

Introduction

Corporate governance is a multi-faceted subject. An important theme of corporate governance is to ensure the accountability of certain individuals in an organization through mechanisms that try to reduce or eliminate the principal-agent problem. A related but separate thread of discussions focuses on the impact of a corporate governance system in economic efficiency, with a strong emphasis shareholders' welfare. There are yet other aspects to the corporate governance subject, such as the stakeholder view and the corporate governance models around the world.

There has been renewed interest in the corporate governance practices of modern corporations since 2001, particularly due to the high-profile collapses of a number of large U.S. firms such as Enron Corporation and Worldcom. In 2002, the U.S. federal government passed the Sarbanes-Oxley Act, intending to restore public confidence in corporate governance.

Factors Influencing Corporate Governance

1. The Ownership Structure

The structure of ownership of a company determines, to a considerable extent, how a Corporation is managed and controlled. The ownership structure can be dispersed among individual and institutional shareholders as in the US and UK or can be concentrated in the hands of a few large shareholders as in Germany and Japan. But the pattern of shareholding is not as simple as the above statement seeks to convey. The pattern varies the across the globe.

Our corporate sector is characterized by the co-existence of state owned, private and multinational Enterprises. The shares of these enterprises (except those belonging to a public sector) are held by institutional as well as small investors. Specifically, the shares are held by:

(a) The term-lending institutions;

(b) Institutional investors, comprising government-owned mutual funds, Unit Trust of India and the government owned insurance corporations;

(c) Corporate bodies;

(d) Directors and their relatives; and

(e) Foreign investors. Apart from these block holdings, there is a sizable equity holding by small investors;

2. The Structure of Company Boards

Along with the structure of ownership, the structure of company boards has considerable influence on the way the companies are managed and controlled. The board of directors is responsible for establishing corporate objectives, developing broad policies and selecting top-level executives to carry out those objectives and policies.

3. The Financial Structure

Along with the notion that the structure of ownership matters in corporate governance is the notion that the financial structure of the company, that is proportion between debt and equity, has implications for the quality of governance.

4. The Institutional Environment

The legal, regulatory, and political environment within which a company operates determines in large measure the quality of corporate governance. In fact, corporate governance mechanisms are economic and legal institutions and often the outcome of political decisions. For example, the extent to which shareholders can control the management depends on their voting right as defined in the Company Law, the extent to which creditors will be able to exercise financial claims on a bankrupt unit will depend on bankruptcy laws and procedures etc.

Mechanisms of Corporate Governance

In our country, their are six mechanisms to ensure corporate governance:

(1) Companies Act

Companies in our country are regulated by the companies Act, 1956, as amended up to date. The companies Act is one of the biggest legislations with 658 sections and 14 schedules.

The arms of the Act are quite long and touch every aspect of a company's insistence. But to ensure corporate governance, the Act confers legal rights to shareholders to:

(a) Vote on every resolution placed before an annual general meeting;

(b) To elect directors who are responsible for specifying objectives and laying down policies;

(c) Determine remuneration of directors and the CEO;

(d) Removal of directors; and

(e) Take active part in the annual general meetings;

(2) Securities Law

The primary securities law in our country is the SEBI Act. Since its setting up in 1992, the board has taken a number of initiatives towards investor protection. One such initiative is to mandate information disclosure both in prospectus and in annual accounts. While the companies Act itself mandates certain standards of information disclosure, SEBI Act has added substantially to these requirements in an attempt to make these documents more meaningful.

(3) Discipline of the Capital Market

Capital market itself has considerable impact on corporate governance. Here in lies the role the minority shareholders can play effectively. They can refuse to subscribe to the capital of a company in the primary market and in the secondary market; they can sell their shares, thus depressing the share prices. A depressed share price makes the company an attractive takeover target.

(4) Nominees on company boards

Development banks hold large blocks of shares in companies. These are equally big debt holders too. Being equity holders, these investors have their nominees in the boards of companies. These nominees can effectively block resolutions, which may be detrimental to their interests. Unfortunately, the role of nominee directors has been passive, as has been pointed out by several committees including the Bhagwati Committee on takeovers and the Omkar Goswami committee on corporate governance.

(5) Statutory Audit

Statutory audit is yet another mechanism directed to ensure good corporate governance. Auditors are the conscious-keepers of shareholders, lenders and others who have financial stakes in companies.

Auditing enhances the credibility of financial reports prepared by any enterprise. The auditing process ensures that financial statements are accurate and complete, thereby enhancing their reliability and usefulness for making investment decisions.

(6) Codes of Conduct

The mechanisms discussed till now are regulatory in approach. The are mandated by law and violation of any provision invite penal action. But legal rules alone cannot ensure good corporate governance. What is needed is self-regulation on the part of directors, besides of course, the mandatory provisions.

Types of Corporate Governance Risk

- Regulatory risk
- Board risk
- Organisational risk
- Shareholder (investment) risk
- Stakeholder risk

Directors are responsible for understanding these risks and ensuring that management takes mitigating action. Corporate counsel, along with other internal units, have a constructive advisory role to play.

Regulatory Risk

Regulatory regimes undergo constant evolution:

➢ *Securities laws:* In recent years, a much stronger focus on insider trading, fraud, market manipulation.

- *Company law:* New focus on director duties, organisation of annual shareholder meetings, statutory derivative actions.
- *Listing rules:* Stricter requirements on financial reporting, independent directors, audit committees, connected transactions, voting by poll, stock options.
- *CG Codes:* Broader and deeper 'soft law' guidelines on Board governance, the role of directors, and auditing.

How many directors of listed companies understand the full extent of these changes? The basic content of the law? And the regulatory and reputational risks that they face?

Many complain that there is 'too much regulation'. But ...

Board Risk

Are companies, especially smaller ones, getting good value from their boards?

- *Board Composition:* Is it appropriate, given the strategic direction and needs of the company?
- *Board Committees:* More thought could be given, in many companies, to the choice of committees, how they operate and what they should achieve.
- *Independent Directors:* If implemented well, they can bring considerable value to a board. But controlling shareholders need to allow them "voice".
- *Director Expertise:* The word "training"is despised by most directors. Yet a good director is an informed director. Knowledge needs to be updated.

Organisational Risk

Are companies investing sufficiently in robust internal controls and creating a culture of accountability?

- *Reporting Lines:* Is the board properly supervising major areas of risk (eg, forex hedging contracts, large M&A transactions)? Does it prioritise risk?
- *Accounting Systems:* Preparation of accounts. Use of information technology. Decisions by senior management on accounting policy.

- *Internal Audit:* Who does it report to—the CFO or chair of the Audit Committee?
- *External Auditor:* Does the company allow its auditor to talk directly to the Audit Committee?

Shareholder (Investment) Risk

Companies like to diversify their shareholder base. But is the board aware of how rapidly the expectations and behaviour of institutional and retail shareholders is changing?

- *Proxy Voting:* Investors need the earlier release of final AGM agendas if they are to vote in an informed way (28 days). They want their votes properly counted ("voting by poll") and the results published.
- *'Pre-emption rights':* Large and dilutive private placements to a select group of investors increases risk to other shareholders.
- *Privatisations/Delistings:* Protection for minority shareholders (eg, approval processes) are weak in much of Asia. Better in Hong Kong, but the PCCW case highlights a legal problem.
- *Related Party Transactions:* Large transactions that benefit the controlling shareholder also increase investment risk and will devalue the company over time. For this reason, one notorious Hong Kong company has a PE of 0.53 and a PBR of 0.05.

An open dialogue with shareholders is good preventative medicine.

Stakeholder Risk

Stakeholder communities and issues are often fluid and also evolve in response to external factors:

- Among investors, the understanding of 'CSR'(corporate social responsibility) is changing and morphing into 'ESG'(environmental, social, governance). ESG puts an explicit governance foundation under CSR.

- Greater focus on the need for investors to incorporate environmental, social and governance ***risks*** into the investment process. For example:

- United Nations Principles of Responsible Investment (UNPRI).
- Greater attention on whether newly listed companies meet requisite environmental and labour standards.
- Global pension funds looking for fund managers who can invest along ESG lines.

Integrating ESG into a company's strategy and operations is the name of the game, but easier said than done.

Systemic Problems of Corporate Governance

- *Demand for information:* A barrier to shareholders using good information is the cost of processing it, especially to a small shareholder. The traditional answer to this problem is the efficient market hypothesis (in finance, the Efficient Market Hypothesis (EMH) asserts that financial markets are efficient), which suggests that the shareholder will free ride on the judgements of larger professional investors.
- *Monitoring costs:* In order to influence the directors, the shareholders must combine with others to form a significant voting group which can pose a real threat of carrying resolutions or appointing directors at a general meeting.
- *Supply of accounting information:* Financial accounts form a crucial link in enabling providers of finance to monitor directors. Imperfections in the financial reporting process will cause imperfections in the effectiveness of corporate governance. This should, ideally, be corrected by the working of the external auditing process.

Recent Corporate Governance Failures

As we have discussed before, the creation of corporate regulation is often linked to perceived failures of corporations and their management to behave in the way society expect them to. Corporate governance is not an exception to this trend, and, as with accounting, different countries may well experience difficulties at different times. For example, the development of British codes of best practice, which began with the Cadbury Committee, can be related to governance scandals such as ***Polly Peck and Coloroll*** in the late 1980s and early 1990s. However, the wave of corporate scandals, mostly in the USA, at the turn of the century has been marked not only by the number of cases but also by the effect they have had on investor confidence and market values worldwide.

The combined impact of various US corporate scandals caused the ***Dow Jones Index*** to drop from a high for 2002 of 10,632 on 19 March to 7,286 on 9 October, wiping out trillions of dollars in market value. Investor confidence in the fairness of the system and the ability of corporations to act with integrity was ebbing. According to a poll in July 2002, 73 per cent of respondents said that Chief Executive Officers (CEOs) of large corporations could not be trusted (Conference Board, 2003). Amongst the many negative effects of this was a worsening of the pension funding crisis caused by the dramatic drop in the value of pension fund assets. It also increased the cost of capital and caused a virtual cessation in new securities offerings. The International Federation of Accountants (IFAC) claims that while there has been a lot of strategic guidance for business, there has been too little said about the need for good corporate governance. These authors emphasize the fact that successful companies were visionary companies, with a long track record of making a positive impact on the world. They did more than focus on profits; they focussed on continuous improvement. They took a long-term view and realised that they were members of society with rights and responsibilities.

However, the long-term view is something of a rarity in many companies. A critical factor in many corporate failures was:

- Poorly designed rewards package
- Including excessive use of share options (that distorted executive behaviour towards the short term)

- The use of stock options, or rewards linked to short-term share price performance (led to Aggressive earnings management to achieve target share prices)
- Trading did not deliver the earnings targets, aggressive or even fraudulent accounting tended to occur. This was very apparent in the cases of Ahold, Enron, WorldCom and Xerox (IFAC, 2003).

Adelphia manipulated its earnings figures for every quarter between 1996 and 2002 to make it appear to meet analysts' expectations. Some of the better known cases of financial irregularities are summarised in following table.

Company	*Country*	*What went wrong*
Ahold	NL	earnings overstated
Enron	USA	inflated earnings, hid debt in SPEs
Parmalat	Italy	false transactions recorded
Tyco	USA	looting by CEO, improper share deals, evidence of tampering and falsifying business records
WorldCom	USA	expenses booked as capital expenditure

In terms of corporate governance issues, Ahold, Enron and WorldCom all suffered from

- Questionable ethics
- Behaviour at the top
- Aggressive earnings management
- Weak internal control
- Risk management
- Shortcomings in accounting and reporting

Corporate governance Failure at Enron

Every time you turn a stone, another worm creeps out. That seems to be the story of the Enron debacle. Not a day goes by without a new expose of wrong doing in the company that one begins to wonder if there is anything in our systems and structure of an enterprise that can prevent such a catastrophe.

Enron is an excellent example where those at the top allowed a culture to flourish in which secrecy, rule-breaking and fraudulent behaviour were acceptable. It appears that performance incentives created a climate where employees sought to generate profit at the expense of the company's stated standards of ethics and strategic goals (IFAC, 2003). Enron had all the structures and mechanisms for good corporate governance. In addition, it had a corporate social responsibility task force and a code of conduct on security, human rights, social investment and public engagement. Yet no one followed the code. The board of directors allowed the management openly to violate the code, particularly when it allowed the CFO to serve in the special purpose entities (SPEs); the audit committee allowed suspect accounting practices and made no attempt to examine the SPE transactions; the auditors failed to prevent questionable accounting.

The use of questionable accounting and disclosure practices, their approval by the board and their verification by the auditors arose from a variety of forces, including:

- Pressure to meet quarterly earnings projections and maintain stock prices after the expansion of the 1990s
- Executive compensation practices
- Outdated and rules-based accounting standards

complex corporate financial arrangements designed to minimise taxes and hide the true state of the companies, and the compromised independence of public accounting firms.

Corporate Governance Failure at Wal-Mart

It has co-filed a shareholder proposal over concerns that Wal-Mart Stores Inc, the US supermarket group, is failing to comply with its own governance standards. Karina Litvack, head of governance and sustainable investment.

- Despite strong policies on paper, Wal-Mart has struggled to implement its standards across its US business.
- 'Weaknesses in internal controls have eroded the company's reputation as an attractive employer and are adding fuel to the fires of Wal-Mart's critics.

- Its failure to deliver on these policy commitments is inhibiting Wal-Mart's ability to expand into new domestic markets.
- Over 'the past several years', it has become increasingly concerned by signs of failure in internal controls that have led to government investigations and class action lawsuits by employees.
- Allegations include requiring employees to 'work off the clock'—during breaks and after shifts—systematic discrimination against women, and alleged questionable tactics to prevent workers from voting for union representation.
- It got off to a promising start in 2005 with expectations of a dialogue with the independent directors on the audit committee. But when this simply withered on the vine, Wal-mart had little choice but to bring concerns about internal controls, labour violations and the erosion of the company's reputation to fellow shareholders.
- Company was not interested in engaging in a productive discussion about how it builds and supports a compliance culture and, as a result, they have joined an international group of large filers led by the New York City Employees' Retirement System to file a shareholder proposal.

Corporate Governance Failure at Satyam

It is one of Corporate India's worst unfolding chapters, What could be the reason behind such a huge collapse? The top level management failed to estimate the intensity of the gangrene in the organization. Questions also arise on the role of the auditors,and how such a magnitude of financial fraud could have gone unnoticed. Corporate governance is a field which constantly investigates how to secure and motivate efficient management of corporations. It has began as a corporate governance issue back in December has now turned into a major financial scandal for the ages in India. The shares of Satyam Computer Services has plummeted more than 90 per cent in trading at the NYSE today, a stark reminder that investors must always cover their backs or else get racked even by the big names in the industry. NYSE today halted trading in Satyam Computer at its bourses in the US as well as in Europe after the Chairman disclosed financial bungling at the Indian IT major.

A business will always have two sides, its not necessary to gain profits everytime, but to sustain in the market the integrity is vital. Every day in some or the other place there is a merger or an acquisition happening, but due to the projected image the co-players in the market are dropping out their plans of taking over Satyam.

Undoubtedly there will be intense focus directed at the other Indian IT Services companies as well.The Satyam corporate governance failure may also make its competitors bolder in terms of acquiring market share created by its fallout, provided the indutsry can regain the trust of the same investors that Satyam has deceived.

From this necessarily brief review of the evidence, and particularly of the sources of failure in financial firms, draw some tentative conclusions. It is important to recognise, however, the evidence base for firm recommendations on corporate governance in financial institutions is thinner than one would like, and certainly not robust enough to offer a standardised set of recommendations valid at all times and in all places.

Principal Conclusions Are

- *First*, that people are more important than processes. Many of the failed firms, or near failed firms which we have encountered, had Boards with the prescribed mix of executives and non-executives, with socially acceptable levels of diversity, with directors appointed through impeccably independent processes, yet where the individuals concerned were either not skilled enough for, or not temperamentally suited to, the challenge role that came to be required when the business ran into difficulty.

- *Secondly,* and in spite of first conclusion, there are some good practice processes worth having. Properly constituted audit committees, and Board risk committees can play an important role, as long as they are prepared to listen carefully to sources of advice from outside the firm.
- *Third,* and this is a foundation stone of the FSA's approach, a regulatory regime built on senior management responsibilities is absolutely essential. In some of the cases we have wrestled with, senior management did not consider themselves to be responsible for the control environment and indeed, in the old pre FSA regime, were able successfully to claim that they were not responsible even if the business failed. So our regulation is built on a carefully articulated set of responsibilities up and down the business. It is important that they are not unrealistic. We do not expect the CEO to check in the bottom drawers of each of his traders for unbooked deal tickets. But we do expect the CEO to ensure that there is a risk management structure and a control framework throughout the business which ought to identify aberrant behaviour, or at least prevent it going on unchecked for any length of time.
- One consequence of this senior management regime, *fourth* point, is that regulators must focus attention on the top level of management in the firm. For the major firms we regulate we insist that our supervisors have direct access to the Board, and that they present to the Board their own unvarnished view of the risks the firm is running, and of how good the control systems are by comparison with the best of breed in their sector. Unfortunately, we find some resistance to this approach. The management of some of our firms want to negotiate the regulators assessment, so that when it reaches the Board it is an agreed paper and sufficiently bland to cause no debate. Well-structured Board, and a confident management, should welcome an independent view, even expressed at

the Board level, which they may challenge and contest if they wish. And non-executive directors should find it helpful to see a knowledgeable view of the institution which does not come from or through its own senior management.

- *Fifth* and penultimate point may not be a popular one. Boards should take more interest in the nature of the incentive structure within the organisation. I am not talking solely about the pay of the CEO, important though that is to get right - as some firms in Britain have recently discovered. Talking about ensuring that the incentives within the firm, and pay is a very powerful one, are aligned with its risk appetite. A number of our most problematic cases have their roots in a misalignment of incentives.
- *Lastly*, no corporate governance system will work well unless there is some engagement on the part of shareholders. Boards are responsible to shareholders. That is the received wisdom in Anglo-American capitalism, at least. But if those shareholders are not prepared to vote their shares, and show little interest in business strategy, then that accountability is somewhat notional, and unlikely to be effective. Certainly regulators cannot hope to substitute for concerned and challenging shareholders, though in some senses they may complement them.

Corporate Governance Failure at Cadbury

Adrian Cadbury, successor to and chairman of the Cadbury Schweppes confectionary group

Mr. Cadbury's visit and interactions with Indian industry triggered the first serious discussions on the subject of corporate governance. All in all, it seemed like a promising new way of looking at the evil that was single promoter-run firms in India then, who, among other things, ran their companies like fiefdoms and were loath to give up control even if their shareholdings were low.

Recognise that it was a not so competitive environment,

the grip of the license raj was still fairly firm and companies and their promoter/founders could pretty much do what they wanted, with public money. The real pain of liberalisation was yet to set in and the Infosys way of boardroom discipline was some way from making its presence felt.

History it seems is repeating itself. Indian companies have exposed themselves to billions of dollars worth of forex derivative contracts over the last few years. Precise numbers are hard to come by and will perhaps never will. What is clear is that companies have taken financial risks they could or should have avoided.

What is clearer is that there was no compelling reason to take these risks. And to that extent, it's a failure of corporate governance and must be treated and then addressed as such. There is of course the other issue of how the Institute of Chartered Accountants or the accounting regulator figuring out how to treat derivative losses as they stand on scores of balance sheets today.

How did it happen? Companies have been steadily stepping up their exposure to currency swaps and the like for at least four years now. Over time, as the stock markets (which bolster sentiment) have held their own and the prospect of any downside risk appeared more and more distant with every passing day, chief financial officers (CFOs) of companies have got braver.

If a company entered into, let's say, a transaction to convert a local currency borrowing into the Japanese yen or Swiss franc borrowing through the swap route, then the company is inducing a risk into the system where there is not. No two ways about that.

Managements ought to have, in the interests of corporate governance, clearly informed their boards of all foreign exchange exposures, the risks arising out of that and the measures to mitigate them were something to go wrong.

Moreover, under the relevant Securities & Exchange Board of India regulations, in the absence of an applicable standard in India for derivatives, the companies' Audit Committees should have examined international standards and disclosed the losses in the Governance report and indicated that these would have been provided for had the country adopted international standards as applicable.

Its possible many companies did keep their boards informed and made the appropriate references in their balance sheets. Though this does seem unlikely, even if they did, no one was watching. It's also possible that some companies are in violation of law. Either way, shareholders must perhaps shoulder some part of the blame.

To conclude is another Enron waiting in the wings? Not quite but it does raise some fundamental questions on what companies do with their shareholders' funds. It's also about how when the good times roll, everyone forgets to look at the figures closely. There is something in the original Cadbury committee definition of corporate governance. "Corporate governance is the system by which companies are directed and controlled."

Getting down to the details of governance, we can focus on five issues

Chairman and CEO: It is considered good practice to separate the roles of the Chairman of the Board and that of the CEO. The Chairman is head of the Board and the CEO heads the management. If the same individual occupies both the positions, there is too much concentration of power, and the possibility of the board supervising the management gets diluted.

Audit Committee: Boards work through sub-committees and the audit committee is one of the most important. It not only oversees the work of the auditors but is also expected to independently inquire into the workings of the organization and bring lapse to the attention of the full board.

Independence and Conflicts of Interest: Good governance requires that outside directors maintain their independence and do not benefit from their board membership other than remuneration. Otherwise, it can create conflicts of interest. By having a majority of outside directors on its Board.

Flow of Information: A board needs to be provided with important information in a timely manner to enable it to perform its roles. A governance guideline of General Motors, for instance, specifically allows directors to contact individuals in the management if they feel the need to know more about operations than what they are being told.

Too Many Directorships: Being a director of a company takes time and effort. Although a board might meet only four or five times a year, the director needs to have the time to read and reflect over all the material provided and make informed decisions. Good governance, therefore, suggests that an individual sitting on too many boards looks upon it only as a sinecure for he or she will not have the time to do a good job.

Corporate Governance: is a multi-faceted subject. An important theme of corporate governance is to ensure the accountability of certain individuals in an organization through mechanisms that try to reduce or eliminate the principal-agent problem. A related but separate thread of discussions focuses on the impact of a corporate governance system in economic efficiency, with a strong emphasis shareholders' welfare. There are yet other aspects to the corporate governance subject, such as the stakeholder view and the corporate governance models around the world.

Conclusion

Most governments have an imperative to try to foster a healthy economy, since this should lead to a better quality of life for all. Inevitably, when the economy suffers as a result of the actions of a relatively small number of people, the government is bound to react. Many initiatives in this area can be seen as a desire to make explicit the obligations that society expects the different actors to fulfill, and provide a framework for penalizing their failure to do so. Such initiatives may also serve as an indication of change in social expectations (sometimes referred to as 'social inflation'), where the generally accepted view of what is acceptable behavior changes. The regulatory changes crystallize a change in the ethical and moral environment. Corporate governance has improved in Asia, but quality varies considerably between markets and companies. Governance failures may start within companies, but ultimately reflect weaknesses at the top. CG risk is a moving target. Directors and managers cannot afford hubris. Directors are responsible for understanding risk and ensuring that managers mitigate it. Corporate counsel has an important and constructive advisory role to play.

References

Bhagat & Black, 'The Uncertain Relationship Between Board Composition and Firm Performance', 54 Business Lawyer).

Business for Development: Fostering the Private Sector . OECD Development Centre. Paris: OECD Publications, 2007 (149-152).

Corporate Governance International Journal, '*A Board Culture of Corporate Governance*', Vol 6 Issue 3 (2003).

Corporate Governance in Development: The Experiences of Brazil, Chile, India, and South Africa. ed. Charles P. Oman. OECD Development Centre and CIPE, 2006.

Crawford, Curtis J. (2007). The Reform of Corporate Governance: Major Trends in the U.S. Corporate Boardroom, 1977-1997. doctoral dissertation, Capella University.

For a good overview of the different theoretical perspectives on Corporate Governance see Chapter 15 of Dignam, A and Lowry, J (2006) *Company Law,* Oxford University Press ISBN-13:978-0-19-928936-3.

Hovey, M. and T. Naughton (2007), A Survey of Enterprise Reforms in China: The Way Forward. Economic Systems, 31 (2): 138-156.

National Association of Corporate Directors (NACD)—Directors Monthly, '*Enlightened Boards: Action Beyond Obligation*', Vol. 31 Number 12 (2007), pg 13.

Nicolas Meisel, Governance Culture and Development (Paris: OECD Publishing, 2004) SourceOECD, 27 July 2007.

Nicolas Meisel, Governance Culture and Development (Paris: OECD Publishing, 2004) SourceOECD, 27 July 2007.

SSRN—Good Corporate Governance: An Instrument for Wealth Maximisation by Vrajlal Sapovadia.

The Disney Decision of 2005 and the Precedent it Sets for Corporate Governance and Fiduciary Responsibility, Kuckreja, Akin Gump, Aug 2005.

6

Improving Corporate Governance for Public Sector Enterprises in India

Emerging Issues and Challenges

Dr. Simanchala Das

Abstract

In view of intensified economic globalization, it has become apparent that the public corporations, one of the keystones of the modern market economy, have become an instrument of economic and social transformation. There is a strong interface between good governance and corporate governance in the context of public enterprises as the latter are often used and perceived as instruments of public policy But there is a good deal of political and bureaucratic influence over the management of public sector undertakings. As a result, the autonomy of the management of the public sector undertakings is often eroded; performance standards are soft, compensation levels low, incentives for performance poor, and 'real' accountability weak. Alleged under-pricing of shares sold, lack of transparency, limited public support for disinvestment and the absence of a common set of objectives between the Government of India and the Disinvestment Commission have been the major challenges. While over the years many countries have implemented successfully the strategy of disinvestment and privatization of public sector enterprises, this tool of public policy still continues to remain elusive and contentious in India. In the developing world, the returns from good corporate governance in these enterprises should exceed those in the private fold. The principles and codes evolved in several countries have furthered the cause of efficiency, transparency and equity particularly in the interest of the shareholders. The Government of India Guidelines to improve corporate governance in PSEs has not been effective for boosting competitiveness. This chapter seeks to examine the changing trends in corporate governance for Public Sector Enterprises in India and explore the emerging issues and challenges in the changed competitive business environment.

Key Words: Globalization, Public Policy, Disinvestment, Privatization, Transparency

Introduction

Corporate governance generally refers to the practices by which organizations are directed, controlled and held to account. Corporate Governance includes the relationships among the many players involved (the stakeholders) in the context of the goals of the company. The principal players are the shareholders, management and the Board of Directors. Other stakeholders include employees, suppliers, customers, banks and other lenders, regulators, the environment and the community at large. The corporate governance structure spells out the rules and procedures for making decisions on corporate affairs. It provides the structure through which the company objectives are set, as well as the means of attaining and monitoring the performance of those objectives. It is about commitment to values, ethical business conduct and transparency. Thus, in essence, corporate governance translates into conducting the affairs of a company in a manner that ensures fairness to customers, employees, shareholders, fund providers, suppliers, the regulators and society as a whole. The absence of good governance structures and lack of adherence to the governance principles increases the risk of public corruption and misuse of entrusted power by the management in public sector.

The importance of good corporate governance has been increasingly recognized for improving the firm's competitiveness, better corporate performance and better relationship with all stakeholders, For that purpose, Indian companies will now be required to make more and more elaborate disclosures than have been making hitherto, for which they are also required to adhere to the uniform and proper accounting standards, as the standards reduce discretion, discrepancy and improves the utility of the disclosure.

The Corporate Governance is a voluntary, ethical code of business concerned with the morals, ethics, values, parameters, conduct and behaviour of the company and its management. The corporate responsibility begins with the directors who are the mind and soul of the organization. The Board is expected to act as conscience-keeper of the corporate vision and mission, and devise the right type of systems for organizational effectiveness and satisfaction of stakeholders.[1] Thus, corporate governance is a system of accountability primarily directed towards the shareholders in addition to maximizing the shareholders' welfare[2]where the debate on disclosure/ transparency issues of corporate governance eventually centers around the proper accounting standards, their practices and issues, as the application of accounting standards gives a lot of confidence to the corporate management and the disclosure would be more effective and ensure the good corporate governance . Thus, the study of practices of accounting standards is an important and relevant issue of good corporate governance in the present environment, as the standards are viewed as a technical response to call for better financial accounting and reporting; or as a reflection of a society's changing expectations of corporate behaviour and a vehicle in social and political monitoring and control of the enterprise.[3]

Corporate Governance involves a set of relationships between a company's management, its Board, its shareholders and other stakeholders.[4] Corporate governance provides a principled process and structure through which the objectives of the company, the means of attaining the objectives and systems of monitoring performance are also set. Corporate governance is a set of accepted principles by management of the inalienable rights of the shareholders as a true owner of the corporation and of their own rule as trustees on behalf of the shareholders. It is about commitment to values, ethical business conduct, transparency and makes a distinction between personal and corporate funds in the management of a company. The primary need of corporate governance is to create corporate culture of conscience and consciousness, transparency and openness.[5]

Evolution of Corporate Governance for Public Enterprises

The debate and effort in the arena of corporate governance has been tilted mostly in favour of the publicly listed and widely held companies. It is possible that three factors have determined this inclination in the debate on corporate governance so far. First was the study of Berle and Means, which had referred to the shifting of control when a company's ownership gets dispersed. The idea underscored the need to create and activate structures and processes by which the owners can ensure appropriate governance and management. The problem identified was not of efficiency of capital in itself or of ownership but the possible divergence in interests between management and the dispersed owner (or some ownership vis-à-vis the rest). The influence of this study on subsequent principles and codes is evident from the arguments for separation of the position of the chairman from that of the chief executive and for induction of independent directors.

The second factor is the Cadbury Committee's report, which has been widely acclaimed and emulated despite its limited set of terms of reference. The London Stock Exchange constituted the committee. The report dealt with the financial issues of the publicly listed companies in the London Stock Exchange. The Cadbury code addressed the prominent concerns of corporate failures and became the mother of all codes in several ways. Most other capital markets and their regulators adopted similar recommendations, albeit, given by locally appointed committees and commissions. The effort, in sum, appears to be towards more efficient regulation through amendments to listing agreements and company laws as well as updated standards of accounting, reporting and disclosures. A comprehensive solution to the Berle and Means propositions appeared to have been found through changes in board structures, processes, shareholder rights, reporting, disclosure standards and legal remedies.

The third factor has been the hope of market efficiency as an ultimate solution to corporate conduct and performance. This implied creation of a market for control of the company and freely entering and exiting owners who make their decisions on the basis of returns. This factor, which has been experiencing a long and bullish run, implies aggressive corporatisation, privatisation and undiluted focus on shareholder value.

These three factors have influenced the environment for good corporate governance in the developed world where capital markets are vibrant. The codes and principles derived from this experience appear to be influencing the developing countries in terms of sensitisation to the need for good governance. This is particularly so in countries where capital markets are expanding briskly. In the process, however, major business/commercial segments of the economies in the developing world are not covered by the corporate governance regulatory net or have found the principles less rewarding in practice. These are agencies, which carry out commercial activities, but operate under the control of the government and those, which are, incorporated public enterprises. In these economies, public enterprises, listed and unlisted, dominate over the private sector listed companies in terms of contribution to GDP, capital employed, income, employee strength, social impact and possibly, as is being asserted lately, even in profitability.

Thus corporate governance has reached centre-stage in the global agenda. The principles and codes evolved in several countries have furthered the cause of efficiency, transparency and equity particularly in the interest of the shareholders. In short, sustainable shareholder value has become the *mantra* for corporate immortality translating eventually into the welfare of the society.

Corporate Governance for Public Enterprises in India

The term "Public Enterprise" has a wider meaning covering various types of state owned/controlled enterprises, the listed and the unlisted government companies, the Central and the state level corporations, public sector banks, insurance and FIs, co-operatives and department undertakings. The equity shares are owned wholly or substantially (51% or more) by the government. Technically, of course, the shares of the Central public sector undertakings are held in the name of the President of India.

The Boards of public sector undertakings, appointed for all practical purposes by the administrative ministry, comprise three categories of directors; (1) functional directors; (2) government directors; and (3) outside directors. But there is a good deal of political and bureaucratic influence over the management of public sector undertakings. As a result, the autonomy of the management of the public sector undertakings is often eroded. Of late, however, things have improved. These undertakings are constrained by various regulations and administrative guidelines. Further, they are subject to the CAG audit and are accountable, to parliament. This leads to an excessive emphasis on observing rules, regulations, and guidelines.

There are about 240 PSEs, leaving aside the financial sector and the departmentally run undertakings. In respect of these enterprises, the Government has been maintaining the 'Arm's length' policy, that means, the ownership functions and there has been an attempt to distinguish between ownership functions and the management functions and the day to day management has been left to the Board of Directors and the administrative Ministries and the department of Public Enterprises. They only issue the guidelines; they just administer the guidelines which are issued for management of these enterprises within the broad policy framework of the Government. The major initiatives taken by the Government have been with respect to professionalization of the Boards, which started as early as in early seventies when the Economic

Administrative Reforms Commission was set up and based upon their recommendations, the professionalization of Boards policy was laid down. Second major reform came in the year 1991 when the Industrial Policy resolution was laid in Parliament and further professionalization of the Boards was announced in pursuance of that policy.

The Department of Public Enterprises (DPE) has issued guidelines on composition of Board of Directors of Central Public Sector Enterprises (CPSEs) According to these guidelines at least one-third of the Directors on the Board of a CPSE should be non-official Directors. The Navratna and Miniratna schemes provide that exercise of the enhanced powers delegated to these CPSEs is subject to the condition that their Boards are professionalized by inducting adequate number of non-official Directors, with minimum four in case of Navratnas and minimum three in case of Miniratnas. The schemes for Navratna and Miniratna CPSEs also provide for setting up of Audit Committees.

In November 2001 DPE issued further guidelines on composition of Board of Directors of listed CPSEs provided that the number of Independent Directors should be at least one-third of the Board if the Chairman is non-executive and not less than 50 per cent if the Board has an executive Chairman. Relevant extracts of Clause 49 of the Listing Agreement with Stock Exchanges issued by Securities and Exchange Board of India (SEBI) form part of the guidelines.

Apart from these instructions of DPE, the CPSEs are governed by the Companies Act, 1956 and regulations of various authorities like Comptroller and Auditor General of India (C&AG), Central Vigilance Commission, administrative Ministries, other nodal Ministries, etc. The Right to Information Act 2005 is also applicable to the CPSEs. The CPSEs fall under the definition of 'State' as provided in Article 12 of the Constitution of India. Further, some principles of corporate governance are already in vogue in public sector because (a) the Chairman, Managing Director and Directors are appointed independently through a prescribed procedure; (b) Statutory auditors are appointed independently by the C&AG; (c) Arbitrary actions, if any, of the Management could be challenged through writ petitions; (d)Remuneration of Directors, employees, etc. are determined on the basis of recommendations of Pay Committees constituted for this purpose; etc.

For the purpose of evolving guidelines on corporate governance, CPSEs have been categorized into two groups, namely: *(i)* those listed in the Stock Exchanges; *(ii)* those are not listed in the Stock Exchanges. In so far as listed CPSEs are concerned, they have to follow the SEBI guidelines on corporate governance. In addition, they may follow those provisions in these guidelines which do not exist in the SEBI guidelines and also do not contradict any provisions in the SEBI guidelines. Each PSE should strive to institutionalize good corporate governance practices broadly in conformity with the SEBI guidelines. The listing of the non-listed CPSEs in the stock exchanges may also be considered within a reasonable time frame to be set by the Administrative Ministry concerned in consultation with the CPSEs concerned. The non-listed CPSEs may follow the Guidelines on Corporate Governance .These guidelines on corporate governance are formulated with the objective that the Central Public Sector Enterprises follow the guidelines in their functioning. Proper implementation of these guidelines would protect the interest of shareholders and relevant stakeholders.

Besides the Central public undertakings, there are several other entities—the state level public enterprises, state controlled co-operatives, organisations created by special statutes, joint ventures of state and central governments, departmental undertakings, companies promoted by developmental financial institutions of the government and the like, which are currently in commercial activities or are pursuing potentially commercial objectives. All these public enterprises have greater potential impact on the society than the private sector due to the higher degree of ripple effect.

Performance of PSEs: The Indian Experience

The top 10 profitable PSEs—BSNL, ONGC, National Thermal Power Corporation, Indian Oil, BPCL, GAIL, Mahanagar Telephone Nigam Ltd, Northern Coalfields, Neyveli Lignite and Nuclear Power Corporation—accounted for 98 per cent of the total profits of all PSUs. Almost half the PSUs operated at less than three-fourth of their production capacities during the year and their inventories continued to rise. Average annual per capita emoluments dipped 12 per cent to ₹1,93,225.But in 2000-2001, they rose by over 30 per cent to ₹ 2,19,672

The government has deliberately neglected its airlines, Indian Airlines (IA) and Air India (AI), for years. The net worth of IA has been wiped off, with the airline having incurred losses in 2002-2003 of Rs 196.56 crore. Air-India is in no better shape—it made operating losses of ₹190 crore in 2002-2003, up from ₹54.53 crore in the previous year. Net gains of ₹49 crore in exchange rate variations and income booked from unutilised services (passenger/cargo) of ₹ 250.6 crore helped the carrier post net profits of ₹134 crore.

But the Kelkar Committee drafted a comprehensive turnaround strategy, which included financial and organizational restructuring, route rationalization and expansion on international routes. The committee sought ₹900 crore in additional equity immediately to help the airline to leverage this for aircraft acquisition. The Naresh Chandra Committee to favoured the infusion of equity in IA and feels that the two issues of divestment and fleet acquisition, which IA desperately needs, should be delinked. AI officials are, however, not exactly thrilled with the committee's suggestion to let foreign airlines avail of AI's unutilized bilaterals. This would result in a lowering of AI's income by ₹500 crore annually, claims one official–yet another instance of how government policy can have a huge effect on its companies. It took almost six years for the government to finally appoint an empowered group of ministers to oversee the privatization process. An exasperated AI official says: "Even now, it is certain that the contract will not be awarded by the April, 2004 deadline set internally."

State-owned telecom companies, on the other hand, have gained considerably from government policy. Bharat Sanchar Nigam Ltd (BSNL) and Mahanagar Telephone Nigam Ltd (MTNL) appear to have been the biggest beneficiaries. For instance, BSNL obtained ₹550 crore and MTNL ₹100 crore by way of compensation in the recently announced compensation package for cellular service companies. Government hand-holding has not done MTNL and BSNL much good, though both have lost market share (from 100 per cent to about 60 per cent), though in an expanding market. According to a Telecom Regulatory Authority of India report, the government-owned companies lost 5 per cent of the market between July and September 2003 to private fixed line service companies. In cellular services, MTNL has garnered only two lakh subscribers in Delhi and Mumbai—private service companies add that many subscribers every month. The exception to the rule: BSNL has become the number two global system for mobile company with over 45 million subscribers within just one year of dialing into the cellular services market.

During the last few years, the government has privatized over a dozen PSUs including CMC Ltd, Videsh Sanchar Nigam Ltd, Bharat Aluminium Company, Modern Foods, Hindustan Teleprinters Ltd, Maruti Udyog, Paradeep Phosphates Ltd, Indian Petrochemicals Corporation Ltd, IBP and Hindustan Zinc Ltd. The sale of the government's 74 per cent stake in Modern Foods to Hindustan Lever in January 2000 set the ball rolling. Modern Food's losses in 1999-2000 stood at ₹ 48.23 crore, including ₹ 35.19 crore as provisions made for previous years. Its finances have improved since then, with the company registering an operating profit before interest and restructuring expenses of ₹1.8 crore in 2002.

The bottom-line of seven of the eight companies in which the government transferred management control have improved. Their profits have shot up by as much as 110 per cent in some cases. Barring the Tata-run Videsh Sanchar Nigam Ltd, whose profits dipped, Modern Foods, Bharat Aluminum Company, CMC, Paradeep Phosphates, Hindustan

Zinc, Indian Petrochemicals Corporation and Hindustan Tele printers have all bettered their performance after the government sold a strategic equity holding in them to private companies. That sure is some track record.

Corporate Governance Abuses In PSUs

It is useful at this point to take a closer look at corporate governance abuses by dominant shareholders in India. The problem of the dominant shareholder arises in three large categories of Indian companies. First the public sector units (PSUs) where the government is the dominant (in fact, majority) shareholder and the general public holds a minority stake (often as little as 20%).

The governance structures of PSUs date back to the days when they were typically wholly owned by the government and were merely an extended arm of the state. These structures allowed the administrative departments in the concerned ministry to exercise virtually complete control over the functioning of these enterprises. It is now evident that these structures are incompatible with the efficient and successful operation of the PSUs in an increasingly competitive and deregulated economy.

It is interesting however to observe how totally irrelevant the Board really is in the governance of the PSUs today. The Board has no role to play in any of the areas where US and UK reformers have sought to strengthen the Board. The Board has very little say in the selection of the CEO or in the composition of the Board. The government as the majority shareholder takes these decisions through the concerned ministry with the help of the Public Enterprises Selection Board. The Board cannot fire the CEO nor can it vary his compensation package. As far as audit is concerned, again the dominant role is that of the Comptroller and Auditor General (CAG). In many PSUs, the Board may still be powerful on paper because the delegation of financial and operating powers to the CEO is very limited. Many operating decisions have to be brought to the Board for decision making. This does not however make for an effective Board because it pushes the

Board into 'managing' rather than 'directing'. The current governance structure allows the Board to play a highly obstructive role if it chooses by opposing the CEO on operational matters.[6] What it does not allow the Board to do is to play a meaningful strategic role since all strategic decisions are taken by the dominant shareholder through the concerned ministry.

The more interesting issue which has not received much attention so far is the potential that exists for conflict between the dominant shareholder and the minority (public) shareholders. There was a well-known case a few years ago where a dispute of several billion rupees arose between two PSUs. One of these was wholly owned by the government while in the other there was a minuscule public shareholding. The government sided with the wholly owned forced PSU and forced the other PSU to pay up the disputed amount, and the impact on the earnings of the concerned PSU was quite substantial. The merits of the dispute apart, there is a serious corporate governance problem in the resolution of the dispute in this manner without either arms' length negotiation or a resort to a judicial process. A minority shareholder could certainly have regarded it as a simple case of enrichment of the dominant shareholder at the expense of the minority shareholder. As government divestiture of minority stakes in PSUs gathers pace, conflicts of this kind would become more frequent and more serious.[7]

Challenges in Checking The Abuses

Regulators face a number of difficulties in tackling the problem of corporate governance abuses by the dominant shareholders. In many cases, it is difficult to decide how far the regulator should go in interfering with the normal course of corporate functioning. Some of these problems are highlighted below. A much talked about regulatory dilemma is that of balancing the rights of minority shareholders against the principle of shareholder democracy. On closer examination, this regulatory dilemma is not as serious as it might appear at first sight. In many ways, the very term shareholder democracy represents a misguided analogy between political governance and corporate governance.

The major weakness in CPSEs was absence of required number of independent directors on the Board of listed government companies and the non-official directors on the Board of unlisted government companies. The absence of independent directors resulted in a number of other instances of non-compliance with clause 49 relating to non-existence of independent directors in the Audit Committee.

Unlike political governance, corporate governance is primarily contractual in nature, and corporate governance is at bottom a matter of enforcing the spirit of this contractual relationship. It is important to bear in mind that the relation between the company and its shareholders and the relation between the shareholders *inter-se* is primarily contractual in nature. The memorandum and articles of association of the company constitute the core of this contract and the corporate law provides the framework within which the contracts operate. The essence of this contractual relationship is that each shareholder is entitled to a share in the profits and assets of the company in proportion to his shareholding. Flowing from this is the fact that the Board and the management of the company have a fiduciary responsibility towards each and every shareholder and not just towards the majority or dominant shareholder. Shareholder democracy is not the essence of the corporate form of business at all. Shares are first and foremost ownership rights—rights to profits and assets. In some cases (non -voting shares for example) that is all there is to it. In other cases, shares also carry some secondary rights including the control rights—rights to appoint the Board and approve certain major decisions. The term shareholder democracy focuses on the secondary and less important part of shareholder rights. Corporate governance ought to be concerned more about ownership rights. If a shareholder's ownership rights have been trampled upon, it is no answer to say that his control rights have been fully respected. Corporate governance abuses perpetrated by a dominant shareholder pose another and far more difficult regulatory dilemma.

Regulatory intervention would often imply a micromanagement of routine business decisions. In a competitive world, highly complex business decisions have to be taken quickly and smoothly. Subjecting a large number of these decisions to the process of regulatory review would make a travesty of a free economy. In the name of ensuring that corporate decisions are taken in the best interests of the company as a whole(rather than just the dominant shareholder), the regulator would end up running the company by remote control. The company would then effectively become an extended arm of the state. Regulatory intervention must perforce be confined to a few clearly defined prohibitions and restrictions that require minimal exercise of regulatory discretion. This approach carries with it the danger that broad prohibitions would also stand in the way of many legitimate business transactions.

Reforming Corporate Governance in PSEs

The past few years have witnessed a silent revolution in Indian corporate governance where Managements have woken up to the power of minority shareholders. In response to this power, the more progressive companies are voluntarily accepting tougher accounting standards and more stringent disclosure norms than are mandated by law. They are also adopting more healthy governance practices. It is evident that these tendencies would be strengthened by a variety of forces that are acting today and would become stronger in coming years.

- *Deregulation:* Economic reforms have not only increased growth prospects, but they have also made markets more competitive. This means that in order to survive, companies will need to invest continuously on a large scale.
- *Disintermediation:* financial sector reforms have made it imperative for firms to rely on capital markets to a greater degree for their needs of additional capital.
- *Institutionalization,* the increasing institutionalization of the capital markets has tremendously enhanced the disciplining power of the market.

- *Globalization:* Globalization of Indian financial markets has exposed issuers, investors and intermediaries to the higher standards of disclosure and corporate governance that prevail in more developed capital markets.
- *Tax reforms:* Tax reforms coupled with deregulation and competition have tilted the balance away from black money transactions. This makes the worst forms of governance less attractive than in the past.

While the above factors may make the capital markets more effective in disciplining the dominant shareholder, there are other things that the government and the regulators can do to enhance this ability by way of:

- *Disclosure of information* is the pre-requisite for the minority shareholders or for the capital market to act against errant managements. The regulator can enhance the scope, frequency, quality and reliability of the information that is disclosed.
- *Regulatory measures* that promote an efficient market for corporate control would create an effective threat to some classes of dominant shareholders as discussed earlier.
- *Reforms in bankruptcy and related laws* would bring the disciplining power of the debt holders to bear upon recalcitrant managements.

Large blocks of shares in corporate India are held by public sector financial institutions who have proved to be passive spectators. These shareholdings could be transferred to other investors who could exercise more effective discipline on the company managements. Alternatively, these institutions could be restructured and privatized to make them more vigilant guardians of the wealth that they control.

In short, the key to better corporate governance in India today lies in a more efficient and vibrant capital market. Over a period of time, it is possible that Indian corporate structures may approach the Anglo-American pattern of near complete separation of management and ownership. At that stage, India too would have to grapple with governance issues like empowerment of the board. Until then, these issues which dominate the Anglo-American literature on corporate governance are of peripheral relevance to India.

Since the power of appointment of directors vests in the Government, some clear decisions at the level of the Government on the induction of a sufficient number of independent directors or non-official directors on the Board is necessary to ensure compliance with clause 49 by the listed government companies and with the Department of Public Enterprises guidelines by unlisted government companies. Audit Committees should normally promote improved systems of risk management and internal control and better financial reporting. An evaluation procedure needs to be put in place to assess the performance of the Audit Committee in promoting better financial reporting. Annual Report of the Board of Directors may contain a section on self evaluation by the Audit Committee in promoting corporate objectives, as a good professional practice. In order to promote good governance in central statutory corporations, the Government may take suitable action for making it mandatory for statutory corporations to form a Board/Members level Audit Committee; and for the positive assertion of the responsibility of Directors'/Members' on the lines of the provisions of the Companies Act, 1956. This is likely to strengthen accountability and commitment of the higher levels of Management towards better systems of risk management and internal controls.

India's progress in public enterprise reform has been modest. The familiar issues of multiple roles of the Government, the agency problem, contractual incompleteness, and information asymmetry continue to affect adversely the potential of this sector. Yet the public enterprises will continue to dominate the economy for several years to come. It is inappropriate to believe that the argument of public vs. private has been settled conclusively so as to imply the gradual disappearance of the state owned enterprise. Despite the notable fatigue and cynicism that has set in, the reality is that Indian public enterprises need reform both in the policy conditions and the internal structures and processes.

The question of privatization of public enterprises arises because of their poor financial and operating performance. Public enterprises in India incur chronic losses, require state financed equity injections and credit from the banking system. Privatization, which is used to mean the transfer of both ownership and control of the firm from the public sector to the private sector, has been viewed as a possible remedy to overcome the malaise of the public sector. Programs to privatize enterprises in transition economies should be evaluated in terms of three broad dimensions: the corporate governance mechanisms they create, the supporting institutions they foster, and the extent to which they create a self-sustaining economic and political reform process. Today, private initiative is being encouraged even in the development of infrastructure like power, roadways, telecommunications, etc. It is believed that privatization will reduce the role of the state, lessen the state's fiscal deficit by decreasing the demand for continued financing of firms from the exchequer, and improve the efficiency and the competitive strength of the public sector enterprises.

Conculsion

The role of corporate governance has vastly changed with the emergence of knowledge capital. Corporate governance is a way beyond disclosures and compliance and calls for a highly innovative and radical framework. Shareholders are not the only owners who matter. Employees have equity well in excess of 70 per cent of the company's assets. Corporations of 21st Century would need to develop strategies to collaborate with employees, customers and suppliers to create value for all stakeholders. With 350 million people still living below the poverty line corporate governance should be treated as an instrument of not only economic transformation but also a means of social transformation. More PSEs should be listed in the stock market to ensure improved corporate governance. The Government should make efforts to list as many PSUs as possible so that they can have more independent directors. The role of the Board and the shareholders should be interactive in nature and the quality of the governance depends upon the level of interface established by them. This can be facilitated by the legal framework which brings into sharp focus on the role of the state in ensuring better corporate governance and its effective monitoring by regulatory and self regulatory agencies in the globalized economy.

References

Chandratre, K.R, "Role of Board of Directors in Emerging Dimensions of Corporate Governance and Impending Changes in Company Law, *The Chartered Secretary,* The Institute of Chartered Secretary of India, New Delhi, May 1997, p. 505.

Guidelines on Corporate Governance for Public Sector Enterprises in India Issued by Dept. of Public Enterprises, Govt. of India, 2007.

Ibid.

Jayanth Rama Varma, Corporate Governance in India: Disciplining the Dominant Shareholder, *IIMB Management Review,* October- December 1997, 9(4), pp.5-18.

Mulla Mansur Ahmad and Mulla Mansur A., Corporate Governance in India: Concept and Evolution, *Third Concept,* Vol.14 (159-160), May-June 2000, p.30.

R.I.Ticker, "Corporate Responsibility, Institutional Governance and the Roles of Accounting Standards" in Michael Bromwich and Anthony G. Hopwood (Eds.), *Accounting Standards Setting, An International Perspective,* Pitman Books Ltd., London, 1983, p.27., Cited in Lele R. K, Jawahar Lal, *Accounting Theory,* Himalaya Publishing House, New Delhi,1996, p.56.

Tiwary, Ojha, Arun Kumar, "Corporate Governance in India: What It Means and What It Needs?"*The Indian Journal of Commerce,* New Delhi, Oct-Dec, 1998, p.154.

7

Corporate Governance and Listed *Companies In An Indian Context*

Dr. Kirti Ranjan Swain

Abstract

The context of the global financial crisis and the wake of financial scandals, corporate governance are especially significant. Listed companies are required to publish financial results on a quarterly basis. The accounting and reporting systems need to be strengthened so as to facilitate quick and accurate reporting. Listing related regulations make it mandatory for companies to share information; broad-base the board of directors to include participation of independent directors; setting up of board sub-committees for reviewing risk, financial information and material events of the company by independent committees. Clause 49 of the Listing Agreement contains the rules on Corporate Governance and it is mandatory for all companies going public to comply with this code. The research paper basically highlighted what are the major aspects of corporate governance and challenges for listing companies.

Introduction

In the present corporate world, corporate governance has been a hotly debated issue and in Indian context; these issues came into force in the last couple of years. The corporate governance code was modeled on the lines of the Cadbury Committee (1992) in the United Kingdom. On account of the interest generated by Cadbury Committee Report, the

Confederation of Indian Industry (CII), the Associated Chambers of Commerce and Industry (ASSOCHAM) and the Securities and Exchange Board of India (SEBI) constituted Committees to recommend initiatives in Corporate Governance. In the Indian context, the need for corporate governance has been highlighted because of the scams occurring frequently since the emergence of the concept of liberalization from 1991 such as the Harshad Mehta Scam, Ketan Parikh Scam, UTI Scam, Vanishing Company Scam, Bhansali Scam, Satyam Scam and so on. In the Indian corporate scene, there is a need to induct global standards so that atleast while the scope for scams may still exist, it can be atleast reduced to the minimum.

Objectives of the Study

The very strong recent public interest in the corporate governance of listing companies has been a vigorous interest in the governance of the companies. The listing companies are looked at a wide variety of forms, structures, processes and practices that can be discerned from agency to agency.

The present study has multifold objectives

1. To analysis the corporate governance practices of listing companies in India.
2. To examine major aspects of corporate governance in listing agreement.
3. To Study governance challenges for India in listed companies.
4. To understand common governance practices if any, in both for listed and unlisted companies.

Corporate Governance and Its Values

Corporate governance, which is the system that helps firms control and direct operations and as a key parts of the governance framework such as audit and finance functions have failed to check the promoter-driven agendas. A well-balanced board of directors, proactive shareholders and swift action against malpractices could restore market confidence.

Various experts indicates that a majority of BSE Sensex companies are perceived to be average in terms of corporate governance practices and also believe that corporate governance norms must be redefined in light of the Satyam episode. Shareholders should ensure that the composition of Board of Directors is a balanced mix of independent directors and management appointees and help keep a check on the internal processes of the company. With shareholder activism on the rise, the proactive role of institutional investors will also make the company management more accountable.

The second annual Corporate Dossier Corporate Governance Seminar asked the seminal question: *What is next for corporate governance in India.*

Business history suggests that it often takes a scandal or unhealthy proportion, really bring into sharp relief the role of ethics and governance in business. The Satyam debacle, India's Enron, has had a profound influence on the Indian business environment and there was a redoubled effort on the part of both the government and other corporations to ensure governance codes were tightened. But what the scandal revealed was that the pressure on companies to maintain their financial performance is enormous. In keeping with that ground reality, the theme for Corporate Dossier's Corporate Governance seminar 2010 was how to link corporate governance with performance. Joseph Massey, MD & CEO, MCX Stock Exchange and co-sponsor for the seminar, set the theme for the morning by asking: How can we balance the two so we don't impede the basic objectives of capitalism? "People do not do certain things due to fear of law and if enforcement is good the fear of law is greater. Then there are also many things people do not do because of fear of God. There is a need to link the two together," said Massey.

The first session of the day, strategic power of corporate governance—had the panelists comparing corporate governance standards in the private sector with PSUs, family managed companies with professionally run companies and large 'A' group listed companies with 'B' and 'C' category companies. PSUs should take a lead in corporate governance," said moderator Deepak Satwalekar, independent director at Infosys. "Corporate governance standards in some 'B' and 'C' category companies on the stock exchange are really lacking," said by Anil Singhvi, Vice Chairman, Reliance Natural Resources.

In recent years, there is an explosion of interest in corporate values like share holder value (Rapport,1986; Copeland, 1994; Jensen, 2000), stakeholder value (Freeman, 1984), customer value (Murphy et al., 1996), business ethics (Velasquez, 1998; Fort, 2001), Corporate social responsibility (Carroll, 1999). But by and large, new value systems have been marketed as general solutions applicable to all kinds of business. These values are building blocks of corporate image. Corporate values are based on high ethical standards of managers and other employees and the firm values must ultimately be derived from the preferences or values of its stakeholders.

Corporate Governance and Listing

Listed companies are required to publish financial results on a quarterly basis. The accounting and reporting systems need to be strengthened so as to facilitate quick and accurate reporting. Besides this, in the run up to an IPO one of the major challenges a promoter will encounter is to learn to share information and give in to a democratic system of decision making. Many of decision making powers enjoyed by Promoter in his capacity as the Managing Director or the Chairman become subject to scrutiny by the Board. Listing related regulations make it mandatory for companies to share information; broad-base the board ot directors to include participation of independent directors; setting up of board sub-committees for reviewing risk, financial information and material events of the company by independent committees. Clause 49 of the Listing Agreement contains the rules on Corporate Governance and it is mandatory for all companies going public to comply with this code.

The company is required to constitute certain committees of the board including the Audit Committee and Remuneration Committee. The audit committee oversees the company's financial reporting process, reviews the financial results including transactions with related parties, internal control systems, utilization of money raised from public in view of the stated purpose and also assesses risks of the Company. It has atleast three members with two-third being independent. The recommendations of this committee are mandatory and generally binding. Atleast four meetings are held each year. The Remuneration Committee recommends the remuneration payable to Executive Directors including the Managing Director. All members of the committee are non-executive members. Listed Companies are required to protect price sensitive information and prevent misuse by insiders. Promoters and Senior Managers are prohibited from dealing in shares of the company if they have access to any information, which if known to public, could have an impact on the share prices. The companies need to follow strict rules with respect to proliferation of price sensitive information. Corporate Governance norms make it mandatory for companies to share with investors its view on the industry and business of the company. It must include Management's view of various matters including industry structure and developments, opportunities and threats, outlook, risks and concerns. Listed Companies are required to protect price sensitive information and prevent misuse by insiders. Promoters and Senior Managers are prohibited from dealing in shares of the company if they have access to any information, which if known to public, could have an impact on the share prices. The companies need to follow strict rules with respect to proliferation of price sensitive information.

The World Bank's corporate governance country assessments are a diagnostic instrument based on the OECD Principles of Corporate Governance and assess the laws, rules, regulations and practices governing the rights and obligations of listed companies, intermediaries and investors in a given country. The current corporate governance assessment for India has found that over the last few years, a series of legal and regulatory reforms have transformed the Indian corporate governance framework and improved the level of responsibility and accountability of insiders, fairness in the treatment of minority shareholders and stakeholders, board practices, and transparency.

The Kumaramangalam Birla Committee to promote and raise standards of corporate governance in its report observed that "the strong Corporate Governance if indispensable to resilient and vibrant capital markets and is an important instrument of investor protection. It is the blood that fills the veins of transparent corporate disclosure and high quality accounting practices. It is the muscle that moves a viable and accessible financial reporting structure." The recommendations of the Committee, led to the inclusion of Clause 49 in the listing Agreement in the year 2000.

The second Committee on Corporate Governance under the Chairmanship of Shri N. R. Narayana Murthy was constituted in October 2002 by SEBI and based on the recommendations of it, SEBI issued a circular on August 26, 2003 revising Clause 49 of the Listing Agreement, to review the progress of the corporate sector in meeting the norms of corporate governance and to determine the role of companies in responding to rumour and other price-sensitive information circulating in the market. In enabled the mechanism of working of transparency and integrity of the market players and participants.

Major Aspects of Corporate Governance and Listing Agreement:

The major aspect of corporate governance in relate with listing agreement are as follows:

- Changes have been made to the definition of 'independent directors'; strengthening the responsibilities of audit committee; improving the quality of financial disclosures and finally; the board as a whole has been tasked with the adoption of a formal code of conduct for senior management and the certification of financial statements issued by the CEO.

- Companies are now required to constitute various committees like a 'nomination committee', 'compensation committee', 'governance committee' and other committees to adhere to corporate governance.
- The law requires the nomination committee of the board to be composed entirely of independent directors, who will be responsible for the evaluation and nomination of board members. In India, the responsibilities of 'audit committee' include scrutiny of the company's annual audited financial statements, appointment of external auditors, interacting with internal auditors and issues relating to internal controls existing in the company.
- Strengthening of disclosure norms for Initial Public Offering (IPO) following the recommendation of Malegam Committee.
- Providing information in the director's report for utilization/end use of funds and variation between projected and actual use of funds.
- Declaration of unaudited quarterly results.
- Requirement of all members of the Audit Committee being financially literate.
- Increase in the powers of the Audit Committee.
- Additional duty on the Audit Committee to review of certain information by the Audit Committee.
- Requirements relating to Audit reports and Audit Qualifications.
- New Requirement of Whistle Blower Policy.
- Change in the Format of reporting to Stock Exchanges relating to Corporate Governance.
- Entitlement to practising Company secretaries to certify the compliance of the conditions of corporate governance

- Mandatory appointment of Compliance Officer for monitoring the share transfer process and ensuring compliance with rules and regulations.
- Dispatch of a copy of complete balance sheet to every investor household and arbitrage copy of balance sheet to all shareholders.

Corporate Governance in Listed Companies—Recommendation of K.M. Birla Committee

Board of Directors: The board of a company provides leadership and strategic guidance, objective judgement independent of management to the company and exercises control over the company, while remaining at all times accountable to the shareholders. The measure of the board is not simply whether it fulfills its legal requirements but more importantly, the board's attitude and the manner it translates its awareness and understanding of its responsibilities

Composition of the Board of Directors: The board of a company must have an optimum combination of executive and non-executive directors with not less than fifty per cent of the board comprising the non-executive directors. The number of independent directors would dependent on the nature of the chairman of the board. In case a company has a non-executive chairman, at least one-third of board should comprise of independent directors and in case a company has an executive chairman, at least half of board should be independent.

Nominee Directors: Institutions should appoint nominees on the boards of companies only on a selective basis where such appointment is pursuant to a right under loan agreements or where such appointment is considered necessary to protect the interest of the institution. When a nominee of the institutions is appointed as a director of the company, he should have the same responsibility, be subject to the same discipline and be accountable to the shareholders in the same manner as any other director of the company.

Chairman of the Board: The role of Chairman is to ensure that the board meetings are conducted in a manner which secures the effective participation of all directors, executive and non-executive alike, and encourages all to make an effective contribution, maintain a balance of power in the board, make certain that all directors receive adequate information, well in time and that the executive directors look beyond their executive duties and accept full share of the responsibilities of governance.

Audit Committee: The need for having an audit committee grows from the recognition of the audit committee's position in the larger mosaic of the governance process, as it relates to the oversight of financial reporting. A proper and well functioning system exists therefore, when the three main groups responsible for financial reporting—the board, the internal auditor and the outside auditors—form the three-legged stool that supports responsible financial disclosure and active and participatory oversight. The committee's job is clearly one of oversight and monitoring and in carrying out this job it relies on senior financial management and the outside auditors.

Remuneration Committee of the Board: The board should set up are remuneration committee to determine on their behalf and on behalf of the shareholders with agreed terms of reference, the company's policy on specific remuneration packages for executive directors including pension rights and any compensation payment.

Disclosures of Remuneration Package: All elements of remuneration package of all the directors i.e. salary, benefits, bonuses, stock options, pension etc. has to be disclosed to shareholders.

Accounting Standards and Financial Reporting: Reporting on accounting based on accounting standards. Reporting should include consolidated accounts in respect of all its subsidiaries in which they hold 51 per cent or more of the share capital. Segment reporting is a must where a company has multiple lines of business. It is important that financial reporting in respect of each product segment should be available to shareholders and the market to obtain a complete financial picture of the company.

Management: The management is subservient to the board of directors and must operate within the boundaries and the policy framework laid down by the board.

Responsibilities of Shareholders: The General Body Meetings provide an opportunity to the shareholders to address their concerns to the board of directors and comment on and demand any explanation on the annual report or on the overall functioning of the company.

Shareholders' Rights: Half-yearly declaration of financial performance including summary of the significant events in last six-months, should be sent to each household of shareholders. A board committee under the chairmanship of a non-executive director should be formed to specifically look into the redressing of shareholder complaints like transfer of shares, non-receipt of balance sheet, non-receipt of declared dividends etc. The Committee believes that the formation of such a committee will help focus the attention of the company on shareholders' grievances and sensitise the management to redressal of their grievances.

Institutional Shareholders: The institutional shareholders take active interest in the composition of the Board of Directors, be vigilant, maintain regular and systematic contact at senior level for exchange of views on management, strategy, performance and the quality of management, ensure that voting intentions are translated into practice and evaluate the corporate governance performance of the company.

Corporate Governance Challenges for India in Listed Companies

The current institutional framework places the oversight of listed companies partly with the Department of Company Affairs (DCA), partly with the Securities and Exchange Board of India (SEBI) and partly with the stock exchanges. This fragmented structure gives rise to regulatory overlap and weakens enforcement. A streamlined regulatory structure would help improve accountability and market discipline. The corporate governance standard is a crucial factor for ensuring investors confidence. The Company Law can take care of the basic requirement of the form of corporate governance structure; SEBI could be concerned with the corporate governance practices on on-going basis. With the SEBI trying to bring some discipline in the stock market especially in terms of greater transparency and disclosure norms, corporate governance in the Indian context at least seems to focus primarily and rightly on the issue of transparency. If corporate governance is concerned with better ethics and principles, it is only natural that the focus should be on transparency. One method of course is the code and another would be the regulatory authorities like SEBI, RBI etc. laying down guidelines so that a certain degree of transparency is automatically ensured. Generally two committees, the ethics committee as well as audit committee, of the board seem to be the instruments by which the board can keep a watch over the actual practices of the enterprise and ensure that the right values are observed and the principles of corporate governance are not violated. The challenge for regulators is to enhance market integrity by enforcing rules and regulations in a professional, timely, transparent and consistent fashion. Regulators should ensure that sanctions and enforcement are credible deterrents to help align business practices with the legal and regulatory framework, in particular with respect to related party transactions and insider trading. This would greatly improve confidence of investors and other stakeholders in the financial markets. Corporate governance rules would make sense, if the regulator demonstrates its ability to book and punish powerful companies that break the laws. New registration requirements make sense if they help the regulator nail fraudsters and market manipulators. And complex disclosure norms for Initial Public Offerings (IPOs) would work if they actually weed out dubious issues. The JPC report of 2002 specifically mentions 15 companies suspected of colluding with Ketan Parekh and other scamsters. One of the biggest weaknesses in SEBI's investigation process is its failure to 'follow the money' to get to the root of market-related fraud. The regulator would need to have access to all the bank accounts where proceeds of market related transactions are deposited and to follow the trail of money when it moves out of those accounts. If the Tax Information Network were able to chip in with income information, it would eliminate the brazen trades through dummy entities as is rampant in regional exchanges. In order to track these shenanigans or to stop them, Sebi needs to enlist RBI's cooperation in its surveillance effort. A key missing ingredient in India today is a strong focus on director professionalism. Directors are expected to know their duties of care and loyalty to the company and all shareholders. However, as that is not always the case, we believe that the law or other regulations should clearly spell out the responsibilities of directors and they themselves should engage in the formulation of their tasks and work procedures.

Conclusion

Corporate governance has assumed vital role and significance due to globalization and liberalization. With the opening of economy and to be in line with WTO requirements, if the Indian corporate have to survive and succeed amidst increasing competition globally, it can only be through transparency in operations. The listed companies constitute the major pool of capitalization and the important segment of the economy namely, capital market in India. It was rightly thought over by the planners to introduce the discipline of corporate governance in listed companies in line with the US model making changes to Indian situations. Despite the regulatory efforts of SEBI and CLB to discipline the corporate, yet we are still in the journey towards the achieving quality in management of companies. On one track reforms take place for tuning of corporate and on the other many scams are unearthed despite many regulations. Good corporate governance would help to maintain the confidence of investors. Hence, not only by just adhering to the regulations on corporate governance a company can contribute to the wealth and health of the investors and society but also by sticking to the principles of ethics and self-discipline.

References

Benjamin E. Hermalin & Michael S. Weisbach, (2007), Transparency and Corporate Governance, Journal of Applied Corporate Finance.

Bhalla V.K, S. Shiva Ram "International Business Environment and Management" 7th Edition, Anmol Publication Pvt. Ltd. New Delhi (2003) pp.655-685.

Cooper, R and Kaplan, R.S (1988), "Measure Costs Right: Make The Right Decisions" Harvard Business Revies, Vol. 66, No. 5, pp. 96-104.

Davis, E. Philip, 2002. "Institutional Investors, Corporate Governance and the Performance of the Corporate Sector," Economic Systems, Elsevier, Vol. 26(3), pp 203-229, September.

Dutta, P. Radner, R. (1999), "Profit Maximization and he Market Selection Proposition", *Review of Economic Studies,* Vol. 66, pp. 769-98.

Edwards, J and Fisher, K (1994), Banks, Finance and Investment in Germany, Cambridge University Press.

Gibson, Michael S., 2003. "Is Corporate Governance Ineffective in Emerging Markets?," *Journal of Financial and Quantitative Analysis,* Cambridge University Press, Vol. 38(01), pp 231-250, March.

Jayati Sarkar & Subrata Sarkar, 2000. "Large Shareholder Activism in Corporate Governance in Developing Countries: Evidence from India," International Review of Finance, International Review of Finance Ltd., Vol. 1(3), pp 161-194.

Joh, Sung Wook, 2003. "Corporate Governance and Firm Profitability: Evidence from Korea before the Economic Crisis," *Journal of Financial Economics,* Elsevier, Vol. 68(2), pp 287-322, May.

Kumar Mangalam Birla Committee on corporate Governance (2000)

Rafael La Porta & Florencio Lopez-De-Silanes & Andrei Shleifer, 1999. "Corporate Ownership Around the World," *Journal of Finance, American Finance Association,* Vol. 54(2), pp 471-517.

Ross Levine, 1997. "Financial Development and Economic Growth: Views and Agenda," *Journal of Economic Literature,* American Economic Association, Vol. 35(2), pp 688-726.

Satheesh Kumar T.N "How Independent are 'Independent' Directors? *Indian Management,* Vol.44, May 2005 pp.66-71.

Shleifer, Andrei & Vishny, Robert W, 1997. " A Survey of Corporate Governance," *Journal of Finance, American Finance Association,* Vol. 52(2), pp 737-83.

Vedpuri A.V, Subramanian and Kaul Vivek "Comingup Short on Disclosures" *Indian Management,* Vol. 43 August, 2004 pp.-60-64.

www.corp-gov.org

www.ebookee.com

www.corpgov.net

www.kesdee.com

www.corpgov.net

8

Corporate Governance
A New Philosophy

Dr. Veershetty G Rathod

Introduction

Corporate Governance has been in place for ages and still in modern day corporate world we see fiascos like Satyam taking place in modern India, which really raises doubt about our financial and commercial ethics, and make us look bad in front of the world. For a non professional corporate governance is almost an alien concept but even they understand something called corporate social responsibility (CSR) and they expect the corporations to be honest and maintain very high level of integrity. Today large number of retail investors are entering in stock market in order to search for better returns or some even invest to earn their bread and butter or may be even for getting future security and in this scenario a big IT and outsourcing player like Satyam gets involved in creative accounting practices or in other words cooking their financial statements, which hurts the financial position of millions of small time investors who not only lose their hard earned money, savings but even their faith in corporate houses and their hope for better future. I term this failure as failure of Corporate Social Responsibility and this happened due to not following corporate governance code. We simply cannot over look the importance of governance of the company and say that it is the governance of country which is more important neither we can term failure of Satyam as failure of central or state government failure the company is more responsible for this fiasco as they were responsible for using public resources and they had the economic responsibility to enhance economic wealth in addition to generate stockholder value, this quote puts the situation more accurately 'The governance of companies is more important for world economic growth than the government of countries.'

Governance is that separate process or certain part of management or leadership processes that make decisions that define expectations, grant power, or verify performance.

Corporate Governance is the system, set of processes, customs, policies, and laws by which business corporations are directed and controlled. The corporate governance structure specifies the distribution of rights and responsibilities among different participants in the corporation, such as, the board of directors, management, shareholders and other stakeholders (include employees, suppliers, customers, banks and other lenders, regulators, the environment and the community at large) and spells out the rules and procedures for making decisions on corporate affairs. By doing this, it also provides the structure through which the company objectives are set and the means of attaining those objectives and monitoring performance.

Introduction to the Concept of Corporate Governance

The concept of corporate governance is poorly defined because it potentially covers a large number of distinct economic phenomenons. As a result, different people have come up with different definitions that reflect their special interest in the field. We will start with widely accepted explanation and will try to develop one of comprehensive explanation of the term. Internationally corporate governance is considered as an—

- International term for responsible corporate management and supervision oriented toward creating long-term added value.

- "Corporate governance deals with the ways in which suppliers of finance to corporations assure themselves of getting a return on their investment", *The Journal of Finance*, ***Shleifer and Vishny.***
- In simple terms, it includes the practices, principles and values that guide a company and its business every day, at all levels of the organization, it is the framework of rules, relationships, systems, and processes within and by which authority is exercised and controlled in corporations. To be more precise it involves series of principles and recommendations to be followed by the management of listed companies.

In this sense, it encompasses the mechanisms by which companies and those in control are held to account. This highlights one fact that in wider sense corporate governance at least covers set of relationships between a company's management, its board, its shareholders and other stakeholders. Based upon this we can easily draw the reference that it is a control measure that can result into overall economic growth and development of an economy plus will generate social justice, if implemented and executed correctly.

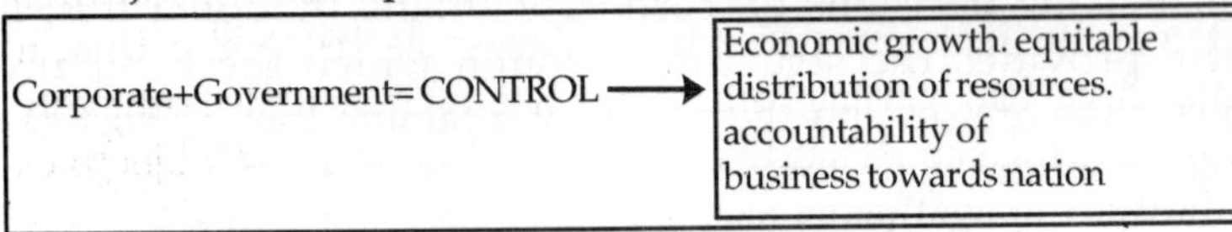

Corporate governance provides a firm foundation for the development of economies. A good corporate governance mechanism improves the health of the corporate sector, thus enhancing national competitiveness. The self-regulatory organizations of various countries have extensive experience in promoting corporate governance and creating a positive corporate governance culture but unfortunately, in India it is not the case.

Indian Scenario

Even much before the issue became a global concern, India was aware of corporate social responsibility (CSR), due to the efforts of organisations such as the Tata Group. (Around 66 per cent of Tata Sons, the holding group of the Tata Group, is today owned by a trust).

Corporate companies like ITC have made farmer development a vital part of its business strategy, and made major efforts to improve the livelihood standards of rural communities. Unilever is using micro enterprises to strategically augment the penetration of consumer products in rural markets. IT companies like TCS and Wipro have developed software to help teachers and children in schools across India to further the cause of education. The adult literacy software has been a significant factor in reducing illiteracy in remote communities. Banks and insurance companies are targeting migrant labourers and street vendors to help them through micro-credits and related schemes.

In June 2008, a survey was carried out by TNS India (a research organization) and the Times Foundation with the aim of providing an understanding of the role of corporations in CSR. The findings revealed that over 90 per cent of all major Indian organizations surveyed were involved in CSR initiatives. In fact, the private sector was more involved in CSR activities than the public and government sectors. The leading areas that corporations were involved in were livelihood promotion, education, health, environment, and women's empowerment. Most of CSR ventures were done as internal projects while a small proportion were as direct financial support to voluntary organizations or communities.

In a survey carried out by the Asian Governance Association, which ranks the top 10 Asian countries on corporate governance parameters, India has consistently ranked among the top three along with Singapore and Hong Kong, for the last eight years.

In another study undertaken by automotive research company, TNS Automotive, India has been ranked second in global corporate social responsibility. State-owned Bharat Petroleum and Maruti Udyog were ranked as the best companies in India. Bharat Petroleum and Maruti Udyog came on top with 134 points each, followed by Tata Motors (133) and Hero Honda (131). The study was based on a public goodwill index and India received 119 points in the index against a global average of 100. Thailand was at the top slot with 124 points.

Several foundations run by corporate houses plan to devise a common strategy to ensure transparency in their social and community development operations, such as tracking spending in and progress of such projects in their annual reports.

The effort is significant because it brings together a wide range of Indian companies to share ideas on innovating sustainable programmes. Among them are Multi Commodity Exchange of India Ltd, Anil Dhirubhai Ambani Group and media company Bennett, Coleman and Co. Ltd.

Audit firm KPMG will partner with them to offer guidance on evaluating corporate social responsibility or CSR programmes—a trend companies are slowly embracing as India's expanding economy contrasts sharply with growing local protests over land for future industrial projects.

The network alliance stems from the first sustainability summit that was organized in January by the Associated Chambers of Commerce and Industry of India.

CSR could prove to be a valuable asset in an age of mergers and acquisitions, especially as it helps companies spread their brand name, The new network will also serve as a common ground to lobby with the government for tax exemptions and safeguard other interests in the future.

Indian companies have made little progress in reporting development projects. And only 48 companies have so far given their commitment to support the United Nations Global Compact, a charter for improving the global business environment through standards, such as labour rights and fighting corruption.

Addressing business leaders in May last year, Prime Minister Manmohan Singh said "Corporate social responsibility must not be defined by tax planning strategies alone. Rather, it should be defined within the framework of a corporate philosophy, which factors the needs of the community and the regions in which a corporate entity functions."

Some say companies have an inherent 'mental block' in reporting development programmes. A recent KPMG study among 27 Indian companies showed that a mere 8 per cent mentioned their social expenditures in their annual reports, and only 25 per cent filed CSR reports at all. But a quarter of them are also signatories of the Global Reporting Initiative, a 10-year-old movement started by an NGO called Coalition for Environmentally Responsible Economies (CERES) and the United Nations Environment Programme. This encourages companies to make voluntary disclosures and lays down framework on improving reporting principles.

"Most companies tend to give to charities than make long-term development commitments. When a company voluntarily opens up for self-evaluation, it creates value for shareholders when competing with other companies," said Parul Soni, associate director of KPMG's Aid and Development Services.

An estimated 100 corporate foundations and 25 foreign firms are involved in CSR activities in India, but statistics on input and output are elusive.

According to Times' Pandey, the Indian corporate sector spent ₹30,000 crore on social expenditure during the last financial year, up from ₹17,500 crore the previous year. Quoting from a government report, he said, companies drew a total exemptions of ₹5,500 crore under income-tax laws last year. These figures, an analyst said, sound improbable as Indian companies still do not distinguish between philanthropy and internal practices to benefit stakeholders such as employees and community.

Companies, too, continue to rely on different models to earmark its social expenditure, making it difficult to measure the overall impact.

For instance, the Steel Authority of India Ltd (SAIL), the country's largest steel company, spent Rs100 crore on CSR last year; this was 2 per cent of its profit after tax, exclusive of dividend tax, according to SAIL spokesperson N.K. Singhal. Yet others, such as Tata Steel Ltd, which runs a 850-bed hospital and rural projects in 800 villages around Jamshedpur, spends an average of 150 crore as part of its annual revenue expenditure.

What eventually makes up for CSR of a company ultimately depends on leadership; as part of company decision, about 66 per cent of Tata Sons, the holding group of the Tata group, is today owned by a trust.

Pharmaceuticals company Jubilant Organosys Ltd, already runs an anti-tuberculosis programme with the government of Uttar Pradesh. Apart from schools and hospitals that are run by trusts and societies, the government, too, is exploring to widen the scope of public-private partnerships to build and maintain schools and hospitals in return for a fixed annuity payment.

Features of Corporate Governance

- Started as economic or financial concept
- Involves lot of parties
- Involves organisational and social objective
- Guiding practices, process and principles
- Used to motivate management to perform better
- Universal approach (world wide acceptance)
- Framework of rules, relationships, systems, and processes
- Implemented at all levels in an organisation
- Tool for benchmarking and controlling performance
- Focuses on long term value addition (profitability, goodwill, brand recognition etc.)

Objectives of corporate governance

As discussed the concept of corporate governance is multi faceted and involves lot of dimensions therefore it covers several objectives rather a wide range of objectives ranging from managing & maintaining Operational transparency to something as simple as following legal mandatory disclosure norms. Next diagram gives us an overview of corporate governance objectives.

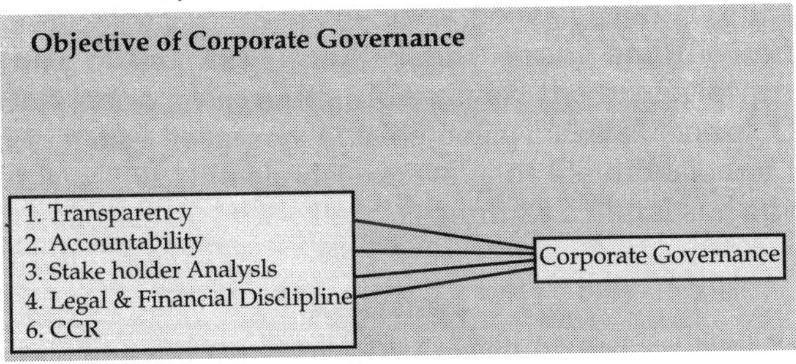

Parties to corporate governance

Parties to corporate governance covers various stakeholders and many more as it has wider coverage and influences society up to a very great extent plus we should not forget that business has greater social obligation as these business houses uses the resources of the society and common men to generate wealth and to earn riches for their shareholders, lastly it should not be forgotten that only those who are directly involved with the business are not the parties whose life is being impacted by decisions of business there are lot of others who may not hold any direct interest in the business but their lives indirectly get influenced and the simple reason for this is the limited availability of resources and opportunity cost so the resources that business is using could have been used for much productive cause and which must have generated more value and benefit for these common men (shadow pricing).

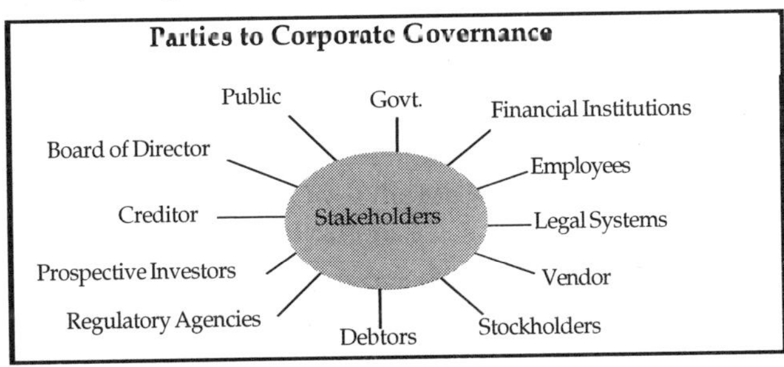

Corporate Governance-Dimensions

Diagram following indicates the several dimensions of corporate governance it also indicates how implementation of corporate governance can help an organisation in improving its operational performance. These dimensions are backbone of corporate governance as well as they are outcomes or working elements of corporate governance process. Corporate Social Responsibility is one of the most important dimensions as it is integral part of corporate governance in addition to being value-enhancing tool for corporate house it is also deliver satisfaction to all parties involved in corporate governance. Corporate governance must encompass and deliver effective resource allocation as by adopting corporate governance a company becomes accountable to society as well as towards other pressure groups. Ethical behavior and entrepreneurial development along with generating economic growth are other dimensions whose importance neither one can ignore nor question.

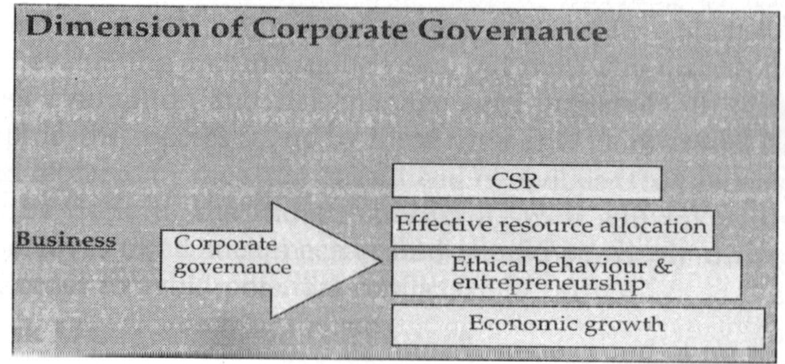

Economic *Vs.* Social Process

The arguments are levelled on corporate governance as only being financial, economic and commercial process but the discussion above especially dimensions of CSR, effective resource allocation, entrepreneurial growth and last but not the least the emphasis on economic growth all indicate that this process is not purely a economic concept or tool though a business is a commercial activity generating profits therefore the emphasis must have been given on commercial or economic aspects of the business in the initial stages of the concept but with time Corporate Governance has been moulded and adequate emphasis on social aspects has also been placed. Presence of various social interest groups in parties of corporate governance and in-depth coverage of social objectives in objectives of corporate governance also proves the point that this concept as on date is no longer a purely economic tool but now it is a mix of economic-social efforts and it is target towards bringing economic social discipline in the arena of business. Inclusion of social elements has made this tool more developed and wider in application. Corporate governance is now a more balanced concept that considers not only economic cost benefit but also uses the social cost benefit analysis as well as use fundamentals like shadow pricing, human resource accounting and social capital audits. It is also important to note that corporate governance is evolutionary; implying that corporate governance practices will evolve in the light of the changing circumstances of a company and must be tailored to meet those circumstances. Corporate governance practices are also bound to be flexible enough to adapt influences of both domestic and international developments.

Instruments of Corporate Governance

Alian Cadbury reports listed the followings tools as instruments for corporate governance:

- Codes
- Principles
- Standards

These instruments provide wider coverage and cover the following areas:

- Shareholders rights and protection
- Shareholders instruments
- Employees and stakeholders right protection
- Company board responsibility
- Transparency of corporate structures and operations, and disclosure of it on time.

Process of Corporate Governance

The process of corporate governance involves four principal activities, which are scheduled as the following:

- Direction—formulating the strategic direction for the future of the enterprise in the long-term (policy and objective)
- Executive action—involvement in crucial executive decisions.
- Supervision—monitoring and oversight of management.
- Accountability—recognizing responsibilities to those making a legitimate demand for accountability.

Attention of Corporate Governance

Corporate Governance issues are receiving greater attention in both developed and developing countries as a result of the increasing recognition that a firm's corporate governance affects both its economic performance and its ability to access long-term, low-cost investment capital. Numerous high-profile cases of corporate governance failure have focused the minds of governments, companies and the general public on this issue.

Moreover, the whole issue of corporate governance became a matter of concern especially because of major shifts in public opinion and societal change on an international scale, together with the strategic requirements of newly emergent forms of business structure, new technologies, globalization and new forms of competition and particularly the investment by the foreign financial institutions in the emerging markets. In other words, when investments take place across national borders, the investors want to be sure that not only is their capital handled effectively and adds to the creation of wealth, but the business decisions are also taken in a manner which is not illegal or involving moral hazard.

Corporate Governance Therefore Calls for four Factors:

(a) To build up an environment of trust and confidence amongst those having competing and conflicting interest;

(b) Transparency in decision-making;

(c) Accountability which follows from transparency because responsibilities could be fixed easily for actions taken or not taken; and

(d) The accountability is for the safeguarding the interests of the stakeholders and the investors in the organization.

Thus, Corporate Governance is a set of rules stipulated for according due weight-age to foster ethical behavior which would help in enhancing the reputation. Thus the code of Governance is as applicable to individuals; the same is also applicable to Corporate.

Development in Corporate Governance in India

In the third century B.C. in the city of Pataliputra (Patna) Kautilya (Chanakya) it's Vizier wrote his celebrated treatise on Statecraft—*Arthashastra* or Law of Economics. History records Pataliputra, the Capital of Mauryan Empire as a ciy "astonishingly well organized and administered according to best principles of Governance."

Kautilya further elaborates on the fourfold duty of a King as:

1. *Raksha*—Protection
2. *Vriddhi*—Enhancement
3. *Palana*—Maintenance
4. *Yogakshema*—Safeguard

The substitution of a state with the Company, the King with the CEO or the Board of a Company and the Subjects with the Shareholders, brings out the spirit of Corporate Governance.

The four principles of Corporate Governance can be elaborated as under:

1. Protecting shareholders wealth;
2. Enhancing the wealth through proper utilization of assets;

3. Maintenance of that wealth and not frittering away in unconnected and non profitable ventures or through expropriation, and above all;
4. Safeguarding the interests of the shareholders.

The development of the Indian corporate sector can be divided into three distinct phases. In the first phase, which lasted from the beginning of independence of the late 1960s, the corporate sector was dominated by 20 family groups who had their beginnings as traders in the pre-independence era and who took a pioneering interest in the industrialization of the country in the post-independence era. These family groups developed strong political connections and took full advantage of the licensing system to control a large portion of the industrial activity.

During the second phase of development from the early 1970s to the mid 1980s, which can be called the socialist phase, these traditional family groups came under intense pressure. During this period a Monopolies Commission was established and restrictions were imposed on the expansion of the family groups, ostensibly with a view to broadening the entrepreneurial base in the country. This phase saw the emergence of a new breed of entrepreneurs who quickly seized the advantage and competed effectively with the traditional family groups. The second phase also saw the emergence of the financial institutions as shareholders in large companies. Access to credit from the financial institutions was based on an important conditionality of converting loans into equity, and this gradually gave the financial institutions a commanding presence in the corporate sector. As the financial institutions were under the control of the government, theoretically the government controlled a large part of India's private corporate sector.

The third phase in the development of the Indian corporate sector began in 1991 with the liberalisation and the globalisation of the Indian economy. With competition replacing the old protected environment, the corporate scene in India is undergoing a sea change. Indian corporations are seriously engaged in re-evaluating their strategy. Under the former regimented system, diversification of the industrial base was dependent on the availability of industrial licenses. When that system withered, the corporations began applying their minds seriously to the concept of core competence. Businesses are being divested, new businesses acquired and efforts being made to scale up operations to international size. This process also raises important issues of corporate governance, including a much greater degree of professionalism of the management. Nonetheless, there are no immediate signs of a clear demarcation emerging between ownership and the management.

Importance of Corporate Governance

- Corporate governance has succeeded in attracting a good deal of public interest because of its apparent importance for the economic health of corporations and society in general.
- Corporate governance provides the structure through which the objectives of the company are set, and the means of attaining those objectives and monitoring performance are determined.
- Corporate governance provides proper incentives for the board and management to pursue objectives that are in the interests of the company and shareholders and should facilitate effective monitoring, thereby encouraging firms to use resources more efficiently.
- The corporate governance structure spells out the rules and procedures for making decisions on corporate affairs.
- Corporate governance is used to monitor whether outcomes are in accordance with plans and to motivate the organization to be more fully informed in order to maintain or alter organizational activity. Corporate governance is the mechanism by which individuals are motivated to align their actual behaviors with the overall participants.

- Corporate governance is a tool for competitive advantage. Normally when we look at the issue of competitive advantage from a managerial point of view, we can look at those factors, which are within the control of the enterprise. This relates to the focus on quality, productivity as well as innovation, which are the basic requirements, in a highly competitive environment. This is needed for getting the competitive edge in a market where the customer is king.
- The corporate governance framework should ensure the equitable treatment of all shareholders, including minority and foreign shareholders. All shareholders should have the opportunity to obtain effective redress for violation of their rights.
- The corporate governance framework recognizes the rights of stakeholders as established by law and encourage active co-operation between corporations and stakeholders in creating wealth, jobs, and the sustainability of financially sound enterprises.
- The corporate governance framework ensures the timely and accurate disclosure of all material matters regarding the corporation, including the financial situation, performance, ownership, and governance of the company. A strong disclosure regime can help to attract capital and maintain confidence in the capital markets. Disclosure also helps improve public understanding of the structure and activities of enterprises, corporate policies and performance with respect to environmental and ethical standards, and companies' relationships with the communities in which they operate.
- Corporate Governance as a catalyst for Organizational Change

Principles of Corporate Governance

- Rights and equitable treatment of shareholders
- Interests of other stakeholders

- Role and responsibilities of the board
- Integrity and ethical behaviour
- Disclosure and transparency

These principles are universal in application and try their level best to provide comprehensive coverage along with complete protection.

Corporate Governance and Firm Performance

In its 'Global Investor Opinion Survey' of over 200 institutional investors first undertaken in 2000 and updated in 2002, McKinsey found that 80 per cent of the respondents would pay a premium for well-governed companies.

They defined a well-governed company as one that had mostly out-side directors, who had no management ties, undertook formal evaluation of its directors, and was responsive to investors' requests for information on governance issues.

Conclusion

With this changing times the need to corporate governance cannot be over emphasized over and above that these troublesome times are the best times to check the effectiveness and efficiency of this practice, this tools has to be provided with razor sharp teeth so incidents like Satyam cannot be repeated and trust of millions of innocent investors and other stakeholders can be maintained in this system.

It has to be remembered that key elements of good corporate governance principles include *Honesty, Trust, Integrity, Openness, Performance Orientation, Responsibility* along with *Accountability, Mutual Respect,* and *Commitment to the Organization Most* important thing is to recognise the fact that corporate governance has succeeded in attracting a good deal of public interest because of its apparent importance for the economic health of corporations and society in general.

References

Corporate Governance by John L. Colley, Jacqueline L. Doyle, Wallace Stettinius, George Logan—Excel Press.

Corporate Governance by Robert A. G. Monks, Nell Minow— Blackwell Publishers; 2nd edition (August 2001).

Corporate Governance: Promises Kept, Promises Broken by Jonathan Macey—University Presses of California, Columbia and Princeton (October 2008).

Corporate Social Responsibility in India—An Empirical Research By Bernadette Dsilva.

CSR Could Prove to Be a Valuable Asset in an Age of M&As, As It Helps Firms Spread Their Brand Name —Maitreyee Handique.

Corporate Social Responsibility is No Longer Just An Addition, It is a Key Differentiator." Prasad Chandra, CMD, BASF South Asia.

9

Risk Management and Corporate Governance

Dr. Niranjan Nayak
Mr. Sidharth Shankar kannugo
Mr. Susanta Ku Mishra

Abstract

We take up the question of potential conflicts between the objective of risk management policies and the objective of maximization of the firm's value or the value of shareholder equity. This question is a timely one, since many firms around the world have a special risk management committee devoted to the evaluation, assessment and management of risk. After the Satyam episode in 2008, several rules of governance have been discussed however, no concrete regulatory changes have taken place. Though actions were taken like dissolving the board, prosecuting the promoters, questioning the auditors, forming probe committees and inspecting the books of accounts of eight Satyam Group companies under the provisions of the Companies Act. What we are trying to point out is, the very provisions need to change. In the wake of the Satyam affair, our government should re-examine its corporate governance framework, and make changes to strengthen it or at least to ensure that the existing frameworks are robustly implemented.

In the financial literature, it is now a widely accepted fact that risk management issues can give rise to conflicts of interest between heads of firms and shareholders, notably when executives hold stakes in the firm or have vested interests in it or remunerated in stock options of the firm. In our opinion, the constitution or physical make-up of the board's risk management committee should be reserved to carefully nominated and recruited directors who are independent and competent and who neither hold any stake nor have any vested interest or option to purchase the firm's shares. Last but not the least, the sad episodes of Satyam and that of Enron certainly raise questions about what standards of risk management and corporate governance exist among businesses the world over, beyond the numerous codes that have been framed and beyond the discussions at seminars and conferences.

Key words: *Corporate governance, risk management, stock options, board of directors, Satyam, Enron, independent director.*

Introduction

We take up the question of potential conflicts between the objective of risk management policies and the objective of maximization of the firm's value or the value of shareholder equity. Any potential conflict would involve serious corporate governance issues, since it is the board of directors which is responsible for deciding on the objectives of the firm's risk management policies and the means employed in achieving such objectives. Among other things, we wonder whether the constitution or physical make-up of the board's audit committee and risk management committee that are mandated to assess risks, should not be reserved to independent directors. This policy has now become a rule for such committees, in accordance with the new regulatiory measures being widely followed the world over in the wake of the Enron affair. Though the governance regime and associated legislative frameworks vary from country to country, similar regulatory measures resulting in a strong regulatory framework should be adopted in the Indian context. In the wake of the Satyam affair, our government should re-examine its corporate governance framework, and make changes to strengthen it or at least to ensure that the existing frameworks are robustly implemented.

This question is a timely one, since many firms around the world have a special risk management committee devoted to the evaluation, assessment and management of risk. In India, guidelines for corporate governance are provided in clause 49 of the listing agreement and also in various sections of the Companies Act. However, as we shall see below, most of these guidelines for corporate governance speak only of regulating the audit committee in matters concerning risk management. This amounts to downplaying the importance of risks in many areas of operations as well as potential conflicts of governance arising from their management. Moreover, no clear explanation is available regarding the abilities of the members of audit and risk management committees. We hold the view that once appointed, the performance and contributions of these members should be monitored and evaluated objectively with peer reviews serving as a means of such evaluations.

Satyam and Corporate Governance

In simple terms corporate governance is about promoting corporate fairness, transparency and accountability. Corporate governance makes the whole structure of the firm more accountable towards each stakeholder, whether it is majority or minority. In the light of the present context, corporate governance can be defined as a control system designed to monitor the firm's operations and the possible conflicts of interests between the different stakeholders. The board of directors is usually considered as one of the most important mechanisms used to achieve such a mission. The principal role of a board of directors is to represent the interests of the firm's stockholders. The board's goal is to maximize the firm's value or the value of its shares. Hence, much attention is focused on the role of the board and of its risk management and audit committees. The constitution or physical make-up of the board and of its different committees is also the topic of much discussion as a large contingent of non-independent members on boards or on board committees may affect the way they operate.

We have chosen to discuss the Satyam case, but the same conclusions could have been drawn with regard to other cases of corporate governance failure: the Enron case, for example.

In September 2008, Satyam had bagged the Golden Peacock Global Award for excellence in corporate governance. However, there wasn't anything award-worthy in December when the incident came into light. The downfall of Satyam has raised numerous questions regarding corporate governance. The manipulation of information by the founding promoter and chairman, B. Ramalinga Raju was notably an important element in the evolution of events preceding the fall of Satyam. What has shocked the world is that the money, that we now call fictitious, had been recorded in Satyam's balance sheets and books of accounts that had been audited by the internationally reputed firm of auditors, PriceWaterhouseCoopers. The entire Satyam episode also raises the question whether the so-called 'Independent' directors on the Satyam board were actually independent or acted in collusion with corrupt company executives.

Even for specialists, it is usually difficult to evaluate a firm's total risk, especially when the financial statements use mark-to-market rather than historical values. It seems that the system as a whole was incapable of detecting the numerous signals which, several months preceding the incident, pointed to problems with management or disclosure or even foretold Satyam's financial troubles. Quite a lot of blame has been heaped on PricewaterhouseCoopers and its partner audit firms who found themselves in a situation of conflict of interest, having assumed an important role by acting as Satyam's auditor. But in our opinion, the Satyam board of directors also failed in its role of protecting the interests of the shareholders, thereby contributing to the downfall of the firm. Several directors of the board were privy to information about the firm's management practices. Therefore, it is completely baffling that none of them was aware of the fact that Satyam was going for the $1.6 billion Maytas acquisition deal. The question that we raise here is whether this was a board decision or a promoter decision.

Another question that we raise is, how the promoter with less than 10 per cent stake made a call on such a huge deal, without approval of those holding the remaining 90 per cent. Even if the articles of association permits a company to carry out a business that it has never done before, the company should seek shareholder approval. The law in place is a bit ambiguous in this regard. Though the Companies Act mandates that a company have articles of association that specify the kind of businesses a firm can do, most Indian companies these days make it broad enough to cover most businesses. So generally shareholder approval is not needed. Yet, if a deal changes the revenue profile of a company, the shareholders should be consulted. If a company is changing its risk profile the shareholder should be informed especially if the new activity has never been done by anyone in the company. Afterall, the way an IT company manages its business is very different from an infrastructure or a real estate company.

The mark-to-market values of shares are strongly influenced by expected future income. Raju manipulated reports on income to influence the value of shares. He exaggerated the revenue, profit, and cash on hand to the tune of over ₹7,000 crores. Researchers have used data from 31 countries to show that manipulations of income by managers are positively correlated with the benefits they receive (on manipulations of data by firms see Lev, B., 2003 and the references in this article). Industry experts are astonished to notice just how silent the board of directors and the audit committee was about the manipulation of data by Raju in the Satyam case. Were the directors of the committee simply incompetent? Were some of them in conflict of interest owing to expected gains or did they have interests in other firms connected with Satyam? As the saying goes, "Quis custodict ipsos custodes?" Who is to guard the guards themselves?

Indeed, the Satyam board was packed with independent directors who are men of standing, and whose abilities no one would ordinarily question: the dean of the prestigious Indian School of Business, a well-known professor of Harvard Business School, a former director of the Indian Institute of

Technology in Delhi, a former cabinet secretary, and the like. However, the lack of financial acumen on the Satyam board was clearly visible. The company admitted in its August 2008 Form 20-F filing with the Securities and Exchange Commission: "We do not have an individual serving on our Audit Committee as an 'Audit Committee Financial Expert' as defined in applicable rules of the Securities & Exchange Commission. This is because our board of directors has determined that no individual audit committee member possesses all the attributes required by the definition 'Audit Committee Financial Expert.'"

The Satyam episode has, ironically, uncovered the largest democracy and the second largest populated country in the world, of having a problem with numbers in terms of finding the requisite number of directors who can exercise their independence while influencing decisions of the board and its constituent committees. The challenge for Indian companies is to come out of the mindset that only well known personalities can be nominated as independent directors. The entire process through which independent directors are identified, nominated and recruited needs a careful introspection. The visibility and market perception or relationships with the promoters should not be the only criteria while choosing independent directors. They should be competent enough to understand as well as comply with the nitty-gritties of corporate governance. As already pointed out, there should also be a system in place that would monitor and evaluate the contributions and performance of the directors.

Obviously, what the Satyam case has put in question is not only the board-mediated relationship between top executives and shareholders. As already pointed out, both the external auditing firm and the internal audit committee have also been called into question. And it is possible that financial analysts and brokers or bankers, lawyers or investors should not be let off the hook either, not to mention regulations which may themselves have introduced distortions. A general analytical framework including all these players should be used to evaluate the situation more realistically (as pointed out by Demski., 2003). No such framework as yet exists, but, in our opinion, the distortions produced by board operations are serious enough to justify the immediate application of corrective measures, even if they are derived from only partial analysis.

As already said, the corporate governance guidelines are enlisted in clause 49 of the listing agreement and also in various sections of the Indian Companies Act. We are of the opinion that, there should be a principle-based approach to compliance (like in the case of the combined code in the UK) where the nature, size and complexities of a business govern compliance and disclosures instead of a standard rules based approach for universal compliance (like in the US and India). Companies in India must have the flexibility to ascertain those aspects which are practical to comply with and others where they can provide suitable and logical explanations for non-compliance. This will enable them demonstrate their true intend to comply. There should also be a clear distinction between corporate governance norms for publicly listed entities and for other forms of businesses involving a relatively limited set of stakeholders. Constituents of corporate governance, including board meetings and agenda code of conduct, ethics, independent directors, CEO succession, performance, risk management etc., should be clearly defined.

We need tighter rules for accounting and corporate governance, including appointment of independent directors by selection committees, and greater oversight from regulatory and government authorities. Separation of audit and consultancy functions at companies, and quicker publication of annual reports is also required. As a matter of fact, integrity and ethical values are not given enough attention in Indian companies, which needs to change, we feel. But what's shocking in the Satyam case is the recognition this company received for its governance even though its board failed to adopt some basic and widespread boardroom best practices.

While all this may be relevant, what is more important in our opinion is: (1) How to salvage Satyam as a company from the effects of this scam? (2) How to prevent the adverse impact of the scam on other IT companies and the Indian stock markets? (3) How to prevent recurrence of this type of incident in future? Nonetheless, we can only hope that from the ashes of Satyam's Golden Peacock rises a phoenix of far superior governance that can not only salvage the company but set a truly worthwhile example of how a world class company should be governed.

New Aspects of Governance

One of our co-authors argues that if the US could have its Enron, why cannot India have its Satyam? The US economy is continuing to grow apace well after the Enron episode. The same can also be said in the Indian context. All this may be acceptable but only up to a point, that point being determined by the extent of 'corruption' prevailing in the society concerned. If we shift our focus to a comparison of corruption prevailing in the US and India, a sphere in which there is not much scope for debate because of the easily demonstrable fact that corruption is much more rampant in our country it is in the US. If this basic premise is accepted, the point can be made that there are many Satyams in the offing and many have already taken place without being detected, which cannot be said of the US in relation to Enron. Further, this cancer is not confined to the corporate sector only. The major difference between Enron and Satyam is that at Enron, the CEO kept shut and the management blew the whistle while at Satyam, the CEO blew the whistle and the management kept shut.

After the Satyam episode in 2008, several rules of governance have been discussed however, no concrete regulatory changes have taken place. Though actions were taken like dissolving the board, prosecuting the promoters, questioning the auditors, forming probe committees and inspecting the books of account of eight Satyam Group companies under the provisions of the Companies Act. What we are trying to point out is, the very provisions need to change. If not, atleast changes should be brought about so that the the efficient implementation of the provisions currently in place becomes possible. As the expert opinion goes, the major problem in the Indian context is the implementation of the law apart from the law itself. However, things were not the same when the Enron episode unfolded in the US. A series of regulatory changes were made in the US in order to improve corporate governance standards in the aftermath of the Enron episode.

The Sarbanes-Oxley Act (SOX) was signed into law by the president of the United States on July 30th 2002. The act amends the 1934 Securities and Exchange Act and enjoins the Securities and Exchange Commission (SEC) to comply with the amendments and to issue regulations and controls designed to protect the public and investors in accordance with the new law. The SEC also studied various recommendations submitted to it by the public as well as by diverse organizations and associations including the NYSE and NASDAQ in view of establishing new regulations. In this sense, the SEC ruled on the minimum requirement for the audit committee: that it must be composed exclusively of independent board members. As required by the SOX, the SEC and the United States Auditor General are also continuing their search to rethink and modify the standards required for listing on the stock exchange.

On 13 February 2002, the SEC asked the New York Stock Exchange to revise its policies with regard to the standards and requirements of governance for firms listed on the exchange. On 1 August 2002, the board of the NYSE approved a number of measures, including the following: (1) Boards of directors must be composed mostly of independent directors. (2) The appointment/governance and remuneration committees must be composed entirely of independent directors. (3) All listed firms must have an audit committee composed exclusively of independent directors and counting at least three members. (4) All listed firms must have an internal audit function. (5) All listed firms must adopt minimum standards of practice and issue directives concerning their corporate governance.

The notion of independence is quite technical and requires a long definition, which, we choose not to get into here. We refer the reader, instead, to the NYSE 2003 entry in the references. But even this reference has nothing specific to say about risk management procedures, except that the audit committee must discuss risk management policies. We here interpret the way different players such as the NYSE perceive the place and purpose of policies for controlling risk evaluation and risk management. In this interpretation, risk management is the responsibility of the firm's management. Management must evaluate and oversee the firm's exposure to different risks. The audit committee must discuss the policies and directives governing the process for evaluating the main risks to which the firm is exposed and the measures to be taken to monitor and control this exposure.

In monitoring and approving their risks, a number of firms, especially financial ones like banks and insurance companies, replace the audit committee with other mechanisms such as the risk management committee. In such cases, the audit committee is no longer obliged to be solely responsible for evaluating and managing risks, but must still discuss the risk evaluation and risk management processes. In other words, the process set up by these firms is to be reviewed but not replaced by the audit committee. We suggest that the same to be done in the Indian context as well. However, the objectives of all such mechanisims should be clearly defined in order to avoid potential conflicts.

Risk Management and Governance

Risk evaluation and risk management instruments are difficult to use and monitor. Understanding them often requires a good grasp of mathematical and statistical concepts apart from a great deal of financial accumen. It is, consequently, not clear that the members of the audit-committee and risk management committee without specialized training would be able to understand their nitty-gritties and even the different speculations presented to them, often in a very rapid and summarised fashion. For example, at the meeting of the

Satyam audit committee on October 17th 2008, five important points were included on the agenda, two of which were linked to presentation by statutory auditors, financial statements and related matters (the list of points discussed and of the committee members present can be found in the minutes of the meeting of the audit committee of Satyam Computer Services Limited). Similarly at the meeting of the Enron audit committee on February 12th 2001, nine important points were included on the agenda, two of which were linked to risk evaluation and risk management (the list of points discussed and of the committee members present is discussed in Healy and Palepu., 2003). Even if the committees in both the cases were composed of leading experts in management and university research, it is unlikely that all these items were explored in depth, particularly those linked to transactions which could have appeared suspicious or tinged with conflict-of-interest concerns.

It is now a well-known fact that risk management issues can give rise to conflicts of interest between corporate executives and shareholders (Smith and Stulz., 1985). Take the example of the risk management of gold mines, which, for several years, has been a topic of detailed study (Tufano., 1996; Dionne and Garand., 2003). The principal random variable linked to the financial risk of firms in this industry is the selling price of an ounce of gold. The three main questions repeatedly asked by the executives of mining companies are the following: (1) Should the selling price be hedged against future fluctuations? (2) If yes, in what proportion? (3) And with what instruments? It is now established that one of the main goal of risk management is to maximize the firm's value or shares. But risk management can also serve to maximize the well-being of executives and this second objective can be in conflict with the first especially when the executives in question have certain vested interest in the organization. This type of conflict can produce problems of governance. Indeed, This finding can be explained by the fact that the value of the stakes held by the executives will increase with the volatility of shares or with the volatility of the firm's value. Even if managers are risk averse with respect to their own wealth, they are risk-leaning or have convex preferences towards the firm's value when they hold stakes in the firm they manage. This is what explains their decisions to engage in fewer risk management activities, since such activities would reduce the volatility of the firm's value and, thus, the value of their options.

A theoretical counter-argument has been presented in the literature that we reviewed (by Carpenter., 2000) which says, holding options has two consequences for the wealth of executives. The first is the one reported above: The wealth of managers will increase with the volatility of stakes because the value of the latter will increase accordingly. The second argument is that the value of the stakes will drop when shares fall in value because the probability of using/selling them will also decline. We thus have an ambiguous relationship between executives holding stakes and risk management activities done by them, but the empirical results mentioned above seem to confirm the dominance of convexity of preferences among managers and the source of conflict of interests between executives and shareholders. Another study shows that firms most active in hedging against risks are those that have the largest number of external directors on their board (Borokhovich,.K.A., Brunarski, K.R., Crutchley, C.E. and Simkins, B.J., 2001) however, these authors did not check whether these directors were independent or in conflict of interest owing to expected gains. A similar ambiguity exists in the case of Satyam.

These results call into question the constitution or physical make-up of risk management committee and the audit committee appointed by boards, since many of the directors may also hold stakes in firms on whose boards they sit or atleast have some form of vested interest or the other. This is a key question, since general risk management policies must be approved and monitored by the board of directors. In our opinion, such committees should constitute competent and independent directors and, above all, it should constitute directors who hold no stakes in the firm or vested interests like options to purchase the firm's shares. It is not obvious that simply regulating the constitution or physical make-up of the risk management committee and the audit committee will suffice to curtail potential conflicts of interest linked to risk evaluation and risk management, especially in firms with committees dedicated to these tasks.

Conclusion

We have documented the fact that risk management policies can give rise to conflicts of interest between shareholders and executives when executives hold stakes in the firm or have some vested interest in it. Some have suggested simply eliminating remuneration in stock options, but there is no guarantee that growth firms will make this a short-term choice, even if Microsoft has recently decided to abolish its program remunerating managers in stock options. *(The Economist,* 13 July 2003; see also *Hall and Murphy.,* 2003). We have also seen that the constitution or physical make-up of the board of directors does have an influence on the risk management policies of firms. The greater the number of external directors on the board, the greater is the number of risk hedging activities undertaken by the firm. Again, the external directors of the firm should be independent of any form of vested interest in it. These different observations lead us to conclude that firms with executives holding stakes or having vested interest or those wishing to maintain their policy of remunerating their executives with stock options should make sure that their board's risk management committee is reserved to carefully nominated and recruited directors who are independent and competent and who neither hold any stake nor have any vested interest or option to purchase the firm's shares. Last but not the least, the sad episodes of Satyam and that of Enron certainly raise questions about what standards of risk management and corporate governance exist among businesses the world over, beyond the numerous codes that have been framed and beyond the discussions at seminars and conferences.

References

Borokhovich, K.A., Brunarski, K.R., Crutchley, C.E. and Simkins, B.J. (2001) "Board Composition and Corporate Investment in Interest Rate Derivatives." Working Paper, Oklahoma State University.

Beverly, B. (2009) "Governance Lessons from India's Satyam" The Boardroom, *Business Week.* http://www.businessweek.com/managing/content/jan2009/ca20090116_465633.htm

Bureau, B.S. (2008) "How Satyam Case Has Dented India Inc's Image" *Business Standard.* http://www.rediff.com/money/2008/dec/19 how-satyam-case-has-dented-india-inc-image.htm.

Carpenter, J.N. (2000) "Does Option Compensation Increase Managerial Risk Appetite?" *The Journal of Finance* 55, 5, 2311-2332.

Demski, J.S. (2003) "Corporate Conflicts of Interest." *The Journal of Economic Perspectives* 17, 51-72.

Dionne, G. and Garand, M. (2003) "Risk Management Determinants Affecting Firms' Values in the Gold Mining Industry: New Empirical Evidence." *Economics Letters* 79, 1, 43-52.

Dionne, G. and Triki, T. (2003) "On Risk Management Determinants: What Does Really Work?" mimeo, Risk Management Chair, HEC Montréal.

Graham, J.R. and Smith, C.W. (1999) "Tax Incentives to Hedge." *The Journal of Finance* 54, 6, 2241-2262.

Hall, B.J. and Murphy, K.J. (2003) "The Trouble with Stock Options." *The Journal of Economic Perspectives* (forthcoming).

Healy, P.M. and Palepu, K.G. (2003) "The Fall of Enron." *The Journal of Economic Perspectives* 17, 3-26.

Lev, B. (2003) "Corporate Earnings: Fact and Fiction." *The Journal of Economic Perspectives* 17, 27-50.

Mahindra Satyam, (2008) "Form 20-F for the Year Ended March 31, 2008" & "Annual Disclosure Document, 2008" http://www.mahindrasatyam.com/

Naavi, (2009) "Satyam Fraud ... Chartered Accountants Call for Action Against PWC" India News. http://www.bloggernews.net/119342.

NYSE, (2003) "Amendment No.1 to the NYSE's Corporate Governance Rule Proposals" http://www.nyse.com/listed.

Ranabir, R.C. (2009) "The Truth Beyond Satyam" *Business Line.* http://sify.com/finance/the-truth-beyond-satyam-news-default-jeguwbhgebb.html.

Rogers, D.A., (2002) "Does Executive Portfolio Structure Affect Risk

Management? CEO Risk-taking Incentives and Corporate Derivatives Usage." *Journal of Banking & Finance* 26, 2, 271-295.

Smith, C.W. and Stulz, R.M., (1985) "The Determinants of Firms' Hedging Policies." *Journal of Financial and Quantitative Analysis* 20, 4, 391-405.

Tufano, P. (1996) "Who Manages Risk? An Empirical Examination of Risk Management Practices in the Gold Mining Industry." *The Journal of Finance* 51, 4, 1097-1137.

10

Media Conglomerates and Corporate Governance

Dr. Suman Kalyan Chaudhury
Dr. Kirti Ranjan Swain
Dr. Niranjan Nayak

Abstract

Do media play any role in corporate governance? This chapter discusses the role of the media in pressuring corporate managers and directors to behave in ways that are 'socially acceptable'. Sometimes this coincides with shareholders' value maximization, others not. It provides both anecdotal and systematic evidence that media affect companies' policy toward the environment and the amount of corporate resources that are diverted to the sole advantage of controlling shareholders. The results have important consequences for the focus of the corporate governance debate and for the feasibility of reforms aimed at improving corporate governance around the world.

Key words: *Media, Corporate Governance, Capital Market, Shareholder Value, Corporation and Securities Law.*

Introduction

Mahatma Gandhi was no bleeding heart socialist and a hard-nosed realist who brought the world's greatest empire to its knees with the sheer force of moral authority. In present scenario, as India Inc. scampers to incorporate 'Inclusiveness' in its agenda, it is worth noting the Father of the Nation's prescient observation on corporate governance, decades before the concept itself was born. "The rich are the trustees of the nation's wealth," he had said. Corporate governance issues have risen to prominence in recent years as a result of corporate scandals and misbehaviour of executives. Companies such as Enron, WorldCom, and Tyco etc. became well known because of massive failures in governance and also governance problems have been evident in media firms as well. In 2002 the U.S. cable TV operator Adelphia was driven into bankruptcy and its controlling family forced out of the company following disclosures of questionable financial transactions between the company and family members. Corporate Governance is one of the critical issues in the present corporate world. For companies Good Governance means securing access to broader based, cheaper capital and investor's commitment to enhanced shareholder value.

Sir Adrian Cadbury was probably the first to enshrine the "Code of Best Practices for Corporate Governance" in 1992 at the behest of the London Stock Exchange. The Kumar Mangalam Birla Report on corporate governance can be a good starting point in Indian industries point of view. There is a solid financial rationale for companies to put in place transparent and practical corporate governance structures in place. The report points out that company with good governance structures are rewarded with higher market valuations. At a time when India Inc. is aggressively expanding its footprint across the globe, it will do well to ensure that corporate boards become truly independent—this will need the induction of more independent directors, of unimpeachable public standing and social conscience, who can nudge managements into initiatives that will make India's growth rates more 'inclusive', without in any way impacting the bottom line. The Mahatma's observation can be the bedrock on which to build such an economic edifice.

Media Conglomerates

In April 1992 the *Wall Street Journal* published a strange advertisement relate with a full-page picture of a silhouette of the board of directors of Sears Roebuck with the title: *"The non-performing assets of Sears."* The advertisement, paid for by shareholder activist Robert Monks, exposed all the directors, who were identified by name, as responsible for the poor performance of Sears' stock. The directors, greatly embarrassed by the advertisement, chose to adopt many of the proposals advanced by Robert Monks. These episodes suggest that the media may play a role in shaping corporate policy. But so many questions are come in the mind. Are these isolated incidents representative of the media's influence? If the media do have such an influence, why do they have it? How does the media's power relate to and interact with other corporate governance mechanisms, such as the legal and competitive environment? In what direction do media influence lead corporate policy?

An answer to these questions is not straightforward. The media play the role of a lever, but a lever used by two very different groups, in first case disenfranchised shareholders and in the second environmentalists. In the first case a dissenting shareholder paid out of his own pocket for an advertisement that communicated his position about the shortcomings of managers and directors and in the second case the television networks included a tape filmed by an environmental group in their regular programming. At the end the outcome is also different. In the first case the public pressure resulting from the advertisement ended up forcing the directors of Sears to increase shareholders' value, an objective they should have pursued to begin with about in the second case it forced them to bow to environmentalist groups, a constituency to which they have no fiduciary duty. Simply the media were instrumental in bringing crucial facts to the attention of customers. As some marketing studies show, a big gap exists between consumer complaints communicated through the press and their willingness to pay. "If there is a dolphin-safe can of tuna next to a regular can, people choose the cheaper product even if the difference is just one penny" (Reinhardt and Vietor 1994a, p. 3). All these questions regarding the media's role receive limited attention in the academic literature.[1] There is no role for information aggregators, which selectively reduce the cost of acquiring information. In the real world the media play this role. People obtain much of their information from the media, which play an important part in selecting which pieces in his survey of the state-of-the-art in corporate finance; Zingales (2000) mentions this as one important force that has been neglected. Skeel (2001) analyzed the role of shaming in corporate law. Baron (1996, 2001) investigated the role of the media in lobbying efforts and in private politics more generally.

The media can play a role in corporate governance in at least three ways:

- Media attention can drive politicians to introduce corporate law reforms or enforce corporate laws in the belief that inaction would hurt their future political careers in the eyes of public opinion, both at home and abroad.
- Media attention could affect reputation through the standard channel that most economic models emphasize. In the traditional understanding of reputation, managers' wages in the future depend on shareholders' and the managers will attend to their interests in those situations where they cannot be monitored.
- Media attention affects not only managers' and board members' reputations in the eyes of shareholders and future employers, but media attention affect their reputation in the eyes of society at large.

Thus the media do play a role in shaping the public image of corporate managers and directors, and pressure them to behave according to societal norms. By reviewing a series of cases where the media do affect corporate policy and to clarify in a theoretical section on issues that determine the impact of the media on corporate behaviour.

---

1 In his survey of the state-of-the-art in corporate finance, Zingales (2000) mentions this as one important force that has been neglected. Skeel (2001) analyzed the role of shaming in corporate law. Baron (1996, 2001) investigated the role of the media in lobbying efforts and in private politics more generally. Djankov and others (2001) studied the effects of the ownership of the press.

Role of Media

In the corporate world media treated as the front line in disseminating impartial news for ensuring transparency and to creating awareness of corporate governance in business houses. Communication between Media and Corporate bodies directly and through efficient public relations or mass communications can be vital to ensure good governance and human rights. Media have a watchdog role to ensure accountability and transparency of corporate sector. Role of Media in pressuring corporate managers and directors to behave in ways that is socially acceptable. Media affects company's policy toward the environment and the amount of corporate resources that are diverted to the sole advantage of controlling shareholders. How the effect of Media on corporate governance explain with necked truth like on 8th March 1988, all the major US networks broadcast a tape of a Panamanian turnabout—the Maria Luisa, killing hundreds of dolphins while fishing for tuna. Media attention can drive politicians to introduce Corporate Law reforms in the belief that inaction would hurt their future political careers or shame them in the eyes of public opinion in the traditional understanding of Reputation, Managers wages in the future depend on Shareholders' and Employer's belief that how much advantage they are going to take of the situation that they are not monitored. Media cannot be important if it is not read. Media freedom and independence also has some impact on the effect it has. Countries with a large newspaper circulation have better environmental responsiveness on average and a religion is major factor affecting literacy of the country and its propensity to read.

It is obvious that journalists give a better coverage to the large companies or those in sectors perceived to have investment potential. As larger companies are regular features of financial reporting, for them managing the press is managing information flows in the most positive way. However, the success of smaller companies depends on communicating their messages into the financial media and managing company reporting with far greater caution and security.

Media and Governance Principles

In recent years public demands for attention to corporate governance have led a number of the leading media companies to create and disseminate guidelines and policies about governance, but their existence is still not common among media firms. The adoption of such statements by companies can be seen as evidence of governance issues and recognition of governance processes to accountability and integrity within the firm. The absence of such policies may indicate that governance is not a significant agenda item for many media companies. However, no research has focused on the characteristics and differences among governance guidelines in media firms or sought to determine whether the existence or non-existence of such policies is related to better financial performance or fewer or increased governance conflicts. A particular governance challenge involves the equality of voting shares. Executives and board members must pay attention to the interests of other shareholders because voting rights proportionally split the equity in the firm, thus providing proportionally equal rights in voting for directors and officers, making changes in the company charter, approving new stock issues, and setting company strategy. Some firms, however, use classified stock that proportionally splits the equity in the firm, but limits or removes voting rights in one or more categories of stock. A large number of media firms have taken explicit action to diminish the influence of ownership by reducing outsiders' voting power through classified stock, including News Corp., Reuters, Tribune Co., New York Times Co., Liberty Media, and Viacom. This unequal division of power is typically seen as evidence of poor corporate governance because a small number of investors hold the most powerful shares and can act in opposition to the majority. Owners of stronger shares in media companies sometimes argue that it provides independence from capital that is necessary to maintain the social, cultural, and political independence.

Media Participation and CG in India

B. Ramalinga Raju, the founder and chairman of Satyam Computer Services, one of the biggest software and services companies of India, road a tiger for years together without knowing where it had been taking him. On 7th January 2009, he confessed to a $1.47 billion fraud on its balance sheet, which he and his brother, Satyam's managing director, had disguised from the company's board, senior managers and auditors for several years (*The Economist*, 2009). Over decades, he had inflated Satyam's profits, even as operations expanded and costs grew up. As the corrective, the government has introduced a new companies' bill which would allow shareholders to pursue class-action lawsuits, but it is supposed to lapse some time before May, 2009. Even if a new government passes the legislation, India's cumbersome courts tend to delay justice to the point of denying it. Even an assertive board and reputed auditors will struggle to stop managers who are determined to cover up their manipulation.

Business families run about half of the 30 companies in the Sensex, India's benchmark stock market index, most of who trace their roots back to the closed economy of the India's past (The Economist, 2009). They will never understand the new rules, until investors collectively protest these practices. Given the context, the role of media in disseminating information and raising public opinion as well as shareholders' activism comes to the forefront. The governance issues in the US or the UK is essentially that of disciplining the managers who have ceased to be accountable to the owners. The problem in the Indian corporate sector is that of disciplining the dominant shareholders and protecting the minority shareholders. Obviously, the problem of corporate governance abuses by the dominant shareholder has to be solved only by forces outside the company itself. Two of such forces are the regulator and the capital market (Varma, 1997). The correction of governance abuses by the regulators would often imply a micro-management of routine business decisions that lie beyond the regulators' mandate or competence. The capital market lacking the coercive power of the regulator has the ability to make business judgments (Varma, 1997). It is hearting that International Finance Corporation (IFC) a member of the World Bank Group, is joining forces with Confederation of Indian Industry to expand the reach of a training program that will help strengthen CG in India. IFC, through its Global Corporate Governance Forum, is tailoring the training program to the Indian Market and working closely with partners on the implementation plan. The programme, created in 2007 by IFC and Securities Exchange Board of India's National Institute of Securities Markets, is designed to reach key players in CG, including board directors, practitioners, academics and the media. Because the media play an important role in raising public awareness and supporting enforcement, program also includes a series of workshops aimed at enhancing journalists' knowledge and reporting techniques concerning CG issues such as transparency and disclosure (www.ifc.org, 2009). So the initiative to integrate media in CG reformation as in the case of IFC is a very pragmatic approach to the issues. Hopefully, the massage would reach the government and other bodies involved.

Corporate Governance and Media Corporate Governance

The implementation of the principles of good corporate governance in media companies, just like any other corporation, implies the acceptation of certain practices that ideally do not bring up special problems. In many cases, the simple acceptation of those generic principles may involve significant advances in the present way to lead the destinies of many companies of the sector. It is necessary to look for the governance approach that fits better the nature of the news activity. In a strict sense, corporate governance refers to the system of internal and external mechanisms that are necessary to solve control problems derived from the separation between company ownership and management. As Becht, Bolton & Röell (2002) (p. 5) point out "at the most basic level a corporate governance problem arises whenever an outside investor wishes to exercise control differently from the manager in charge of the firm. Dispersed ownership magnifies the problem by giving rise to conflicts of interest between the various corporate claimholders and by creating a collective action problem among investors". So a good system of corporate governance would be the one that gets the managers to take the best possible decisions in order to maximize the value of the company for its owners, through internal mechanisms as well as external means. As Tirole (2001) states, a corporate governance system tries to solve "an adverse selection and a moral hazard problem. A good governance structure is then one that selects the most able managers and makes them accountable to investors" (p. 3). Since the Hutchins Commission established the principle of social responsibility of media in relate with Corporate Governance and News Governance in Media Companies and according to the widespread current acceptance of their public transcendence, it seems clear that news companies fit perfectly into models of corporate governance which harmoniously integrate the focus on the stakeholders and the maintenance of the public trust demanded by the exercise of the journalistic duties. The principles of news governance in the corporate management systems of journalistic companies in order to encourage promote and reward the fact that the "professional agents" would act to the advantage of society, according to their honesty and professional ability.

Conclusion

Papers have focused on the important role of the media in shaping corporate policy and governance. It argued that the Media selectively reduce the cost of acquiring and verifying information. While the strength of the impact of the media depends on their credibility, the direction of their net effect depends on special norms and values, but much more research is needed before coming to a conclusion on this matter. Media are important in Shaping Corporate policy and should not be ignored in any analysis of a Country's Corporate Governance System. In the corporate world, one of the most important fact is that media plays an important role with governance. The good news is that even countries with inadequate laws and malfunctioning judicial systems can experience some of the benefits of better governance if the pressure of the press is sufficiently strong and the norms support good governance. Moreover, the extent of press influence may be largely outside policymakers' control. Our analysis of the ultimate determinants of the diffusion of the press indicates that these lie in a country's cultural and ethnic tradition.

References

A.H. Belo Kimberly Clark, PepsiCo, Circuit City Activity, New York, NAA, 1976.

Berle Jr., A.A. & Means, G.C. (1932). The Modern Corporation and Private Property. New York: Macmillan.

Bikki, Jaggi, Corporate Social Performance: Objectives, Measurement and Reporting.

Blankenburg, W. & Ozanich, G. (1993). The Effects of Public Ownership on the Financial Performance of Newspaper Corporations, *Journalism Quarterly*, 70, 68-75 (Spring).

CalPERS [California Public Employees Retirement System] (2004). Governance Principles, Policies and Practices. http://www.calpersgovernance.

Carlsson, R (2001). Ownership and Value Creation—Strategic Corporate governance in the New Economy. New York: John Wiley and Sons.

Chandler Jr., A.D. & Daems, H., Eds. (1980). Managerial Hierarchies:Comparative Perspectives on the Rise of the Modern Industrial Enterprise. Cambridge, Mass.: Harvard University Press.

Chang, K.K. & Zeldes, G.A. (2002). How Ownership, Competition Affect Papers' Financial Performance, Newspaper Research Journal, 23(4),101-107.

Clark, T. (2004). International Corporate Governance: A Comparative Approach. Routledge.

Coase, R.H. (1937). The Nature of the Firm, Economica, 4, 386-405.

Companies, B.M. (1982). Who Owns the Media? Second Ed. White Plains, NY: Knowledge Industry Publications.

Cranberg, G., Bezanson, R. & Soloski, J. (2001). Taking Stock: Journalism and the Publicly Traded Newspaper Company. Ames: Lowa State University Press.

Cyert, R.M. & March, J.G. (1963). A Behavioural Theory of the Firm. Englewood Cliffs, N.J.: Prentice Hall.

Demsetz, H. & Lehn, H. (1985). The Structure of Corporate Ownership: Causes and Consequences, Journal of Political Economy, 93(6), 1155-1177.

Dow Jones J. C. Penny, American Express, Sprint, SBC Communications.

Dutta Gupta, A.K., Perspective of Social Audit Management Accountant, Vol. 25, No. II.

Eisenhardt, K. M. (1989). Agency Theory: An Assessment and Review, Academy of Management Review, 14(1), 57-74.

Gannett UAL Co., Kellogg, S C Johnson & Son, Coca Cola, American Express.

Ghosh , T.P., Structure of Corporate Social Reporting in India, Vol. No. XLIII, Part IV, No.165.

Jawaharlal, Contemporary Accounting Issues, Vision Books, New Delhi, 1988.

Karassen V., Ramnathan, "Towards a Theory of Corporate Social Accounting", Accounting Review, April, 1976, pp. 284-90

OECD (2003). Survey of Corporate Governance Developments in OECD Countries. http://www.oecd.org/dataoecd/58/27/21755678.pdf.

OECD (2004). OECD Principles of Corporate Governance, Draft Revised Text. http://www.oecd.org/dataoecd/19/29/23888981.pdf.

Picard, R.G. (1994). Institutional Ownership of Publicly Traded U.S. Newspaper Companies, Journal of Media Economics, 7(4):49-64.

Picard, R.G. (2002). The Economics and Financing of Media Companies. New York: Fordham University Press.

Porwal, L.S., Accounting Theory—An Introduction, Tata McGraw Hill Publishing Co. Ltd., New Delhi, 1986.

Sarbanes-Oxley Act (2002). Public Law 107-204 (HR3763). Representation of 100 Leading Advertisers from 1988 to 2000 Company Leading Advertisers on the Board.

Seidler, Lee J. and Lynn L. Seidler, Social Accounting Theory: Issues and Cases, Melville Publishing Co., Los Angles, 1975.

Tripathi, P.C. and P.N. Peddy, "Principles of Management", Tata McGraw Hill Publishing Company Limited, New Delhi, 1991.

Index

❑❑❑